Clothing for Liberation

Clothing for Liberation

A Communication Analysis of Gandhi's Swadeshi Revolution

Peter Gonsalves

www.sagepublications.com
Los Angeles • London • New Delhi • Singapore • Washington DC

First published in 2010 by

 SAGE Publications India Pvt Ltd
B1/I-1 Mohan Cooperative Industrial Area
Mathura Road, New Delhi 110044, India
www.sagepub.in

SAGE Publications Inc
2455 Teller Road
Thousand Oaks, California 91320, USA

SAGE Publications Ltd
1 Oliver's Yard
55 City Road
London EC1Y 1SP, United Kingdom

SAGE Publications Asia-Pacific Pte Ltd
33 Pekin Street
#02-01 Far East Square
Singapore 048763

Published by Vivek Mehra for SAGE Publications India Pvt Ltd, typeset in 10.5/12.5 pt Adobe Garamond Pro by Diligent Typesetter, Delhi and printed at Chaman Enterprises, New Delhi.

Library of Congress Cataloging-in-Publication Data

Gonsalves, Peter.
   Clothing for liberation: a communication analysis of Gandhi's swadeshi revolution/Peter Gonsalves
      p. cm.
   Includes bibliographical references and index.
   1. Gandhi, Mahatma, 1869–1948—Political and social views. 2. Swadeshi movement. 3. Clothing and dress—Political aspects—India—History—20th century. 4. Khadi—Political aspects—India—History—20th century. 5. Communication in politics—India—History—20th century. 6. Symbolism in politics—India—History—20th century. 7. Social change—India—History—20th century. 8. Nationalism—India—History—20th century. 9. India—Economic policy. 10. India—Politics and government—1919–1947. I. Title.

DS481.G3G5856   954.03'56—dc22   2010   2010001069

ISBN: 978-81-321-0310-3 (HB)

The SAGE Team: Elina Majumdar, Pranab Jyoti Sarma, Amrita Saha and Trinankur Banerjee

To
communicators and educators of
PEACE

Contents

List of Tables and Figures

Tables

Figures

List of Photographs and Images

List of Abbreviations

AICC	All India Congress Committee
AISA	All-India Spinners Association
AIVIA	All India Village Industries Association
Autobiography	*An Autobiography: The Story of My Experiments with Truth*
CWMG	*The Collected Works of Mahatma Gandhi*
Congress	Indian National Congress
Hind Swaraj	*Hind Swaraj and other Writings*
MMG	*The Mind of Mahatma Gandhi*
PSEL	*The Presentation of the Self in Everyday Life*
SSA	*Satyagraha in South Africa*

Foreword

There was hardly anything charismatic about him; he was 'a little man with a poor physique', shy and diffident to a fault, and when he spoke in public, the could barely be heard. He was certainly no great orator, nor would he have stood out in a crowd. As a lawyer and journalist there was hardly anything spectacular about him. Indeed, Mohandas Karamchand Gandhi was the unlikeliest of men to lead the Freedom Movement of one of the world's most populous nations.

Yet, this frail and 'half-naked fakir' came to be followed by the millions in India and South Africa and by sheer dint of his message of love, truth and non-violence, succeeded in bringing the mighty British Empire to its knees. That message was largely embodied not so much in what he said or wrote but rather in the way he carried himself and lived his life, identifying himself with the poorest of India's millions. As he would often reiterate in his speeches and newspaper articles: My Life is My Message.

An integral part of that life and that message was the clothes he wore, and he wore the bare minimum even when he met royalty and participated in the Round Table Conferences in London. There is an abundance of scholarly work on Gandhi as a writer and journalist, as a mass communicator par excellence, but little discussion in the Gandhian literature on the role that cloth and clothing played in the Mahatma's message of non-violence and liberation, except perhaps in the context of the Swadeshi Movement.

This study by Peter Gonsalves fills that lacuna. It explores the transformations that took place in Gandhi's life and message (frequently interchangeable as he often made clear) as he 'experimented with truth' and matured into a *satyagrahi* and the acknowledged leader of the Freedom Movement. Gonsalves focuses on the clothes that Gandhi wore and the symbolism of such attire at each stage of his life. He traces the journey of this apostle of non-violence through the changes in his attire from his childhood in a *bania* family in Gujarat, through his years in England and South Africa until later as he plunged into India's freedom struggle.

Gonsalves' elaborate analysis of Gandhi's clothes as mass communication is conducted in terms of three 'western' theoretical frameworks: semiotics and structuralism (Roland Barthes), cultural anthropology, particularly symbolic interactionism (Victor Turner) and Erving Goffman's theory of performance in the daily lives of individuals.

This is an unusually challenging approach. One would have expected him to take the well-beaten path of looking at the clothes which the Mahatma wore within the tradition and history of Indian/Hindu philosophy and culture, particularly the tradition of the *sanyasi* or *rishi* or the guru, where 'renunciation' was the key. That is the Indian tradition in which Gandhi's sartorial preferences make most sense, a tradition that goes back to the Buddha and the ancient seers.

But no, Gonsalves sticks his neck out and dares to apply three Western theories related to critical cultural studies to the dissection of the meaning and influence of Gandhi's clothes. I am inclined to believe that the application does work fairly successfully.

The significance of this study lies in its major contribution to our understanding of the vital role that non-verbal communication, with particular reference to Gandhi's use of clothing, played in the Freedom Movement. The study is also a contribution to the vast literature on the impact of the Mahatma and his life on freedom and peace movements worldwide.

Over the last two decades or so, Gonsalves has been passionately promoting courses on media education and peace education in South Asian secondary schools. He has conducted about 40 teacher-training workshops on media education across the region. His workbooks and writing have guided teachers in their pedagogy, based on participatory learning. This latest scientific study of his is a significant contribution to the discipline of communication and cultural studies.

Keval J. Kumar, PhD
Director
Resource Centre for Media Education and Research
Pune

Acknowledgements

Many thanks to the directors of the following institutions in India that have allowed me the generous use of their facilities: Gandhi Smarak Sangrahalaya, Manibhavan, Bombay Sarvodaya Mandal and Nirmala Niketan.

I also wish to thank GandhiServe Foundation, *The Hindu*, Nehru Memorial Museum and Library and the British Library Board for the photographs and illustrations.

Introduction

We live in a 'forest of symbols'.[1] Our environment is suffused with meanings that crave our attention—some more powerfully than others, some more intelligently designed to achieve their ends. Some symbols inspire, others debase, most are mediocre.

There are a few rare symbols, however, which are imbued with the capacity to energise millions in the pursuit of sublime goals. They invite a commitment that draws their adherents to a calling far beyond themselves, to total dedication even to the point of giving their lives. My purpose is to explore one such symbol in a defining moment in history: clothing, as used by Mohandas Karamchand Gandhi (1869–1948) throughout his archetypical non-violent campaign to liberate India from British rule.

Through his Swadeshi Movement,[2] Gandhi chose to dress and clothe his fellow countrymen and women in a specific type of cloth called *khadi*. This choice was not fortuitous. Through it he not only wanted to eradicate unemployment, but also empower, unite and liberate his people from centuries of foreign domination. The choice gave to clothing—a conventional form of non-verbal communication—a historical, political, economic, social, psychological, cultural and moral significance that had no precedence and has no parallel. In terms of scale, context, method and consequence, the dress revolution he initiated transformed a disunited and submissive mass of over 383 million[3] people into one independent nation, free from imperial control—a phenomenon that heralded the beginning of the end of British imperialism across the world.[4] Jawaharlal Nehru, India's first Prime Minister, was so moved by the impact *khadi* had on the masses that he extolled it as the 'livery of India's freedom'.[5]

Yet, it must be admitted, Gandhi's insistence on spinning and wearing *khadi*, was one of the most misunderstood initiatives he had undertaken.[6] When he proposed the 'spinning franchise' at the All India

Congress Committee in 1924—that Congress members spin yarn instead of paying their regular membership fee—Nehru, the then AICC secretary, was among those who were deeply angered to the point of submitting his resignation.[7] Motilal Nehru, his father, marched out of the hall with a good number of followers just before the proposal was put to vote.[8]

There were discordant voices from articulate members of society as well. Aurobindo Ghose called the spinning franchise 'a tremendous waste of energy'.[9] Rabindranath Tagore thought that in deciding to use or refuse cloth of a particular manufacture, Gandhi was trespassing into economics, a field he was not competent to deal with.[10] Nirad C. Chaudhuri considered the Mahatma's demands 'extreme...crude and irrational'.[11] Even Samuel Evan Strokes, an American missionary, a good friend of Gandhi and an enthusiastic spinner himself publicly declared: 'Not only my reason but all my instincts, [...] rebel at the idea of a spinning franchise.'[12]

In this book I argue that a non-verbal communication perspective on Gandhi's sartorial choices may help us see what his contemporaries were, perhaps, unable or unwilling to recognise: the *symbolic potential* behind the home-manufacture and exclusive use of *khadi* for Indian unity, empowerment and independence.

At the outset it must be noted that the term 'clothing' is used here in a broader than ordinary sense. It means attire, apparel, dress or costume, but it also covers the pre-garment phase as cloth, textile or woven fabric. Emphasis is also placed on the particular scope for which the potentialities of cloth and clothing were used in the case under study: not merely as functions of bodily protection, adornment or identification, but also as *symbols of liberation*.

The chapters are horizontally, theoretically and vertically structured. The first presents Gandhi's diverse communication skills in a broad sweep. It serves as a backdrop to the chapters that follow, but it can also open up new possibilities for further research in Gandhian communication. Chapters 2 to 4 are detailed analyses of Gandhi's evolution in the personal and social use of clothing from the perspective of Western communication theories. The theoretical frameworks underpinning these studies are the semiotics of Roland Barthes, the anthropology of performance of Victor Turner and the dramaturgical analysis of Erving Goffman. These three chapters that form the bulk of the book are as demanding as they are rewarding: demanding in terms of technical language and rewarding for the new insights they offer on Gandhi and *swadeshi*. The book concludes with a brief in-depth presentation of what may be called a 'Gandhian approach to symbolisation' for socio-political change.

No attempt has been made to bring together the insights in a comprehensive conclusion. Each chapter is an independent exploratory tour that the reader is invited to experience and evaluate on its own merits. Each opens a new window that offers a refreshing perspective on the panorama of Gandhi's communication ability. The thread that connects the chapters is Gandhi's non-verbal communication through clothing.

The use of Western theories to analyse Gandhian communication may strike the reader as self-contradictory: a *videshi*[13] analysis of the Swadeshi Revolution! On looking deeper, one will note that such an exercise in a globalised world is not only legitimate and necessary, but also mutually enriching to both the elements in the dialectic. On the one hand, the applicability of the theories is challenged beyond their original contexts; on the other hand, the power and audacity of Gandhi's sartorial strategy comes alive as never before. It must be noted, however, that the application I have attempted in this book is not exhaustive. It could help unravel the significance of other equally interesting variables in the struggle for Indian independence.[14]

Finally, I wish to explain the reason for my research on Gandhi's symbolic use of clothing. I have always been fascinated by the power of non-verbal communication to change the hearts and minds of audiences in ways that spoken and written words cannot. As an educator, I was amazed at the extremely sophisticated levels of audio–visual creativity that impact young minds, so I decided to promote mass media literacy among teaching staff. The manual, *Exercises in Media Education*, was a practical response to this deeply felt need.[15]

The more I was drawn into an all-India media education network, the more I felt the importance of emphasising quality over technique. It was not enough to appreciate mass media critically, or to learn the skills of employing them creatively and profitably. The multi-polarised Indian ethos needed principled communicators, ready to encourage a unity in diversity and the promotion of equal dignity for all citizens. The violent communal riots that accompanied the 1990s well into the new millennium only strengthened my resolve to redesign a media education for peaceful and responsible citizenship.

I did not have to look far for an appropriate model. I had always admired, although superficially, the courage of that one diminutive individual who brought down an Empire by the strength of his truth. As soon as the opportunity presented itself, I plunged into a three-year historical and communication research on Gandhi's atypical choice of a 'clothing for liberation'.

I am deeply indebted to my companions on this journey— Professors Tadeusz Lewicki, Franco Lever, Bernard Grogan, Philomena D'Souza and Ivo Coelho—for their availability, encouragement and valuable suggestions.[16]

Dr Keval Kumar is one of the first among scholars to highlight the importance of analysing the communication impact of Gandhi's clothing. I am grateful to him for consenting to write the Foreword.[17]

It is my hope that the chapters in this book be a modest contribution to the growth of peace communication research.

Notes

1. The phrase is borrowed from the title of the book by Victor Turner, *The Forest of Symbols – Aspects of Ndembu Ritual* (Ithaca: Cornell University Press, 1986).
2. The word *swadeshi* means 'of one's country'. The Swadeshi Movement was a campaign for autonomy and self-sufficiency by promoting the use of resources available in one's own territory rather than depending on what is foreign.
3. The 1940 census reports released by the Government of India reveal that the total population of Indians on the subcontinent (under the British Raj and under Indian states and agencies) was 383,643,745.
4. India (including today's Pakistan and Bangladesh) was the first of the coloured races of the world to demand and obtain independence from the British Empire. Twenty-three years later, 40 other nations obtained theirs—from Burma in 1948 to Tonga in 1970. See complete list at: World Facts and Figures, 'Independence': http://www.worldfactsandfigures.com/country_independence.php (24 May 2007).
5. D.G. Tendulkar, *Mahatma*, volume 6 (Delhi: Publications Division, 1951–54/ 1960), 20.
6. In the eyes of his contemporaries, Gandhi seemed too sure of the benefits of the *khadi* movement for Indian independence. For instance, after calling a halt to the first all-India *satyagraha* due to the outbreak of violence at Chauri-Chaura, he sent out this message from his cell at the Sabarmati Jail: 'Place Khadi in my hands and I shall place Swaraj in yours.' *CWMG*, vol. 23, 86.
7. Nehru, *An Autobiography*, (New Delhi: Penguin Books, 2004), 134.
8. *Ibid.*

9. Aurobindo Ghose, *India's Rebirth* (Paris: Institut De Recherches Evolutives, 1994) in Rahul Ramagundam, *Gandhi's Khadi: A History of Contention and Conciliation* (Hyderabad: Orient Longman Private Limited, 2008), 180.
10. Sabyasachi Bhattacharya, ed., *The Mahatma and the Poet* (New Delhi: National Book Trust, 1997), 90.
11. Nirad C. Chaudhuri. 2000, 'The Autobiography of an Unknown Indian', in *Gandhi's Khadi*, ed., Ramagundam, (Mumbai: Jaico, 2000), 179.
12. Asha Sharma and Nandini Sharma, *An American in Gandhi's India: The Biography of Satyanand Stokes* (Indiana: Indiana University Press, 2008), 191.
13. *Videshi* means 'foreign', the opposite of *swadeshi*.
14. Barthes's theory, for instance, can be used to unravel the deeper historico-cultural significance of more symbols in the Swadeshi Revolution besides cloth and clothing, such as, the *charkha*, the salt march or Gandhi's notion of *Ramarajya*.
15. Peter Gonsalves, *Exercises in Media Education* (Bombay: Tej-prasarini, 1999).
16. Tadeusz Lewicki, PhD (Durham University) is former Dean of the Faculty of Communications, Salesian University, Rome; Franco Lever, PhD, is the present Dean of the same Faculty; Bernard F. Grogan, STL, BA (London University) is a professional educator and translator; Philomena D'Souza, PhD (Tata Institute of Social Work, Bombay), is former Principal of Roshni Nilaya—School of Social Work, Mangalore; Ivo Coelho, PhD (Gregorian University) is former Principal of Divyadaan—Salesian Institute of Philosophy, Nashik.
17. Dr Keval Kumar is a retired professor of Communication and Journalism, Pune University. He was Director of Symbiosis Institute of Media and Communication, Pune, and is currently Adjunct Faculty Member at the International School of Business and Media, Pune. See his pioneering article entitled 'Gandhi's Ideological Clothing', in *Media Development*, 31, no. 4 (1984): 19–21.

1

Gandhi the Communicator

I hold my message to be far superior to myself and far superior to the vehicle through which it is expressed. It has a power all its own, and I hope it will produce an impression on the youth of India. Whether it will produce an impression in my lifetime or not, I do not care, but my faith is immovable, and as the days roll on and as the agony of the masses becomes prolonged, it will burn itself into the heart of every Indian who has a heart to respond to the message. You must understand, that at a time of my life when I should be enjoying my well-earned rest, I am not going about from one end of the country to the other for nothing. It is because I feel within myself with increasing force every day the strength of my conviction that I must try until the end of my days to reach it to as many ears and hearts as possible.[1]

M.K. Gandhi

The Indian struggle for independence was unlike any other in world history.[2] Most major political revolutions were armed struggles that involved the mobilisation of a core group belonging to a particular section of the population. The Indian revolution is distinguished by its unique combination of *non-violent subversive action* and the *participation of millions* that cut through all sections of a heterogeneous population consisting of different races, languages, cultures, castes, classes and creeds—all spread over a geographically vast and complex terrain.

There is a third element, however, that identifies the Indian revolution as singular and exceptional: it was led by the charisma and integrity of *one solitary individual*, Mohandas Karamchand Gandhi.[3]

Although it is impossible to scientifically determine the extent of Gandhi's influence over the masses, three eyewitness accounts are indicative: Krishnalal Shridharani, a researcher of *satyagraha*[4] and one of the first to promote it as a scientific technique for socio-political change, gives us a glimpse of Gandhi's influence in his interviews with scores of participating Indian villagers. On asking them 'What is *Satyagraha*?' he received the same reply: 'Satyagraha is *Gandhi's* way of fighting the British Raj.'[5] Dr Harold H. Mann, the Director of Agriculture in Bombay from 1921–1927, was asked by Sir Thomas Jones, Secretary to the British Cabinet, 'How many of the 310 millions in India have heard of Gandhi?' Dr Mann replied, 'Three hundred and nine millions.'[6] Lord Mountbatten, the last British viceroy in India, referred to Gandhi as the 'one-man boundary force'[7] who brought to a halt the Hindu–Muslim riots in Bengal simply by his presence and his fasting.

One of Gandhi's fundamental insights was that Indians themselves were responsible for their own subjugation: 'We wore Manchester cloth and this is why Manchester wove it.'[8] It was therefore incumbent on Indians to put aside their many differences and to unite in order to shake off the shackles of subjugation. For this, he planned the Swadeshi Movement. But he needed to draw larger sections of India's unarmed humanity into the vortex of the struggle. He needed to raise awareness beyond the confines of the Congress Party. He had to inject into the urban and rural illiterate masses a new mentality—fearlessness, a passion for independence and a belief in their own capacity to achieve it. He was convinced that only a communication strategy that was methodologically planned, hermeneutically relevant, creatively symbolic, morally disciplined, geographically extensive and founded uncompromisingly on *satya* and *ahimsa* would succeed. This holistic, principled communication has marked Gandhi out 'for generations to come'[9] as 'that rare great man held in universal esteem, a figure lifted from history to moral icon [...] [who] stamped his ideas on history, igniting three of the century's great revolutions—against colonialism, racism, violence'.[10]

Natural Communication Skills

If we look back at the young Mohandas, we are struck with incredulity. He was hardly the kind of material from which one would expect to see the flowering of a great communicator. He was short in stature, of wheatish complexion, with teapot ears,[11] without exceptional qualities to attract attention. His teachers considered him a 'mediocre student', very shy and introvert. In his autobiography, he notes:

> This shyness I retained throughout my stay in England. Even when I paid a social call the presence of half a dozen or more people would strike me dumb […]. It was impossible for me to speak *impromptu*. I hesitated whenever I had to face strange audiences and avoided making a speech whenever I could. Even today I do not think I could or would even be inclined to keep a meeting of friends engaged in idle talk.[12]

Strangely, Gandhi's greatest obstacle to communicating was to be his greatest communication asset. He was the first to acknowledge it. It saved him from the tendency to engage in futile conversation and from the temptation to make an impression on his audiences.

> My hesitancy in speech, which was once an annoyance, is now a pleasure. Its greatest benefit has been that it has taught me the economy of words. I have naturally formed the habit of restraining my thoughts. And I can now give myself the certificate that a thoughtless word hardly ever escapes my tongue or pen. I do not recollect ever having had to regret anything in my speech or writing. I have thus been spared many a mishap and waste of time.[13]

Thanks to his shyness, he was able to consolidate inner convictions and develop self-discipline that lent credibility to his vast repertoire of communication skills. Bharati Narasimhan, a member of the editorial team of the hundred-volume project, *Collected Works of Mahatma Gandhi* (henceforth *CWMG*) adds: 'One can hardly believe that a bumbling student and a nervous lawyer could go on to become such an effective journalist and communicator.'[14]

Verbal Communication Output

Gandhi's verbal output is astonishing. A cursory glance at the indices of the *CWMG* will reveal an enormous number of speeches, comments, interviews, discussions, letters, replies, diary notes, telegrams, reports, messages, petitions, appeals, articles and even books. He wrote and spoke fluently in English, Hindi and Gujarati, which implies that many of the items included are meticulous translations into English. The *CWMG* is, perhaps, one of the largest collections of writings and speeches by any single individual. It was Pandit Jawaharlal Nehru who set in motion the process of collecting and presenting in one series all Gandhi's writings and transcripts of his speeches. He called the compilation 'a duty we owe to ourselves and to future generations'.[15] The project took 38 years to complete.

Today, the *CWMG* fill a hundred volumes that contain approximately 500 pages each, making a total of over 50,000 pages. The project began in 1956, and the main series of 90 volumes was brought to a completion under the prime-ministership of Smt. Indira Gandhi in the year 1983–84. Another 10 volumes—seven supplementary volumes, one index of subjects, one index of persons, one compilation of all the prefaces—came out by the year 1994.

These volumes cover the period from 1884 to 1948, or nearly 64 years of Gandhi's very active public communication in his 79-year lifespan. The aim of the editors has consistently been 'to reproduce Gandhi's actual words as far as possible'.[16] They make no claim to completeness or finality as further research in the course of time may reveal more documentation.

The *CWMG* also include Gandhi's five books: *Satyagraha in South Africa* (1899), *Sarvodaya* (1908), *Hind Swaraj* (1909), *Autobiography* (last revision 1925) and *Ethical Religion* (1930). A large number of his writings appeared first in journals and in course of time were published as separate booklets by the Navajivan Trust, with Gandhi's blessing.[17]

Dr Rajendra Prasad, India's first President, pays homage to Gandhi in the introduction to the *CWMG* as follows:

> Here are the words of the Master covering some six decades of a superbly human and intensely active public life—words that shaped and nurtured a unique movement and led it to success; words that inspired countless individuals and showed them the light; words that explored and showed a new way of life; words that emphasized cultural values which are spiritual and eternal, transcending time and space and belonging to all humanity and all ages.[18]

Gandhi's verbal output was the fruit of an overwhelming desire to communicate, to dialogue, to express himself and to stay in touch with people. The urge was so strong that he cultivated the capacity to write incessantly by using both his hands!

The Question of Language

English was the official language of India under the British rule. Yet it was spoken by a very small section of the population, particularly by England-returned graduates and students of missionary-run institutions in the cities. It was the language used by the Indian National Congress to overcome difficulties in its multilingual membership and to maintain relations with the Government.

Gandhi radically changed this. He proposed Hindi as the common national language of India since it was the most widely used language of the people in a majority of provinces.[19] Despite his inability to speak it fluently, his first intervention in the Congress meeting at Lucknow on December 1916 was in Hindi. To those who did not speak or understand it, he requested that they learn Hindi within a year, or run the risk of being ostracised by the majority when it becomes the *lingua franca*, because, 'I know [it] will be the *lingua franca* when *swaraj* is granted to the whole of India.'[20]

Gandhi was adamant on choosing Hindi. He considered it hypocritical to oust the British while clinging to their language and their culture. The fight for *swaraj* had first to be a struggle for *swadeshi*, and intrinsic to *swadeshi* was the question of appreciating a 'home' language instead of the language of the colonisers. He himself made efforts to learn and perfect his fluency in Hindi and apologised for having insisted on speaking it despite his mistakes 'because even if I speak a little of English, I have the feeling that I am committing a sin'.[21]

Notwithstanding these convictions, Gandhi himself used English whenever he thought it necessary and important. He dreaded the language when he studied law as a 19-year-old in England. But he soon came to master it to the point of writing in English on the important issues of the day. Years later, he would edit three newspapers in English—*Indian Opinion*, *Young India* and *Harijan*. He used it to rebut the British Raj at every step with exactitude, firmness, respect and originality.[22] He economised on vocabulary, meticulously choosing words to express himself in a clear, forceful idiom. He perfected it to the level of an art, distinguishing the subtle nuances that even Englishmen sometimes overlooked.[23] Edward Thompson,[24] a professor at Oxford University shares this experience:

> Perhaps, his unsurpassed command of English idiom comes partly from this perfect control over his mind. The hardest thing in our language for a foreigner is our prepositions. I never met an Indian who had mastered them as Gandhi has. I learnt this during the Round Table Conference, when two or three times he asked me to draft some statement for him. If you are a professional writer, you try to be careful about your prepositions, and I admit that I took a deal of trouble over this drafting. Mr Gandhi would glance over my work, and would make just one subtle prepositional change—you might (if you did not know English from the roots of your mind) think the change was a trifle. But it did its work. Perhaps it left a loophole (and politicians are suspected of linking loopholes). Anyway, it changed my meaning into Mr Gandhi's meaning. And our eyes, as they met and each of us smiled at the other, showed that we both knew that this had happened.[25]

Gandhi also wrote and spoke in Gujarati, his mother tongue. Some of these writings include his articles in *Navajivan* and *Harijan Bandhu*. His *Autobiography* was first written in Gujarati and published in *Navajivan* in a serialised version entitled, *Atmakatha*. According to Kanhaiyalal M. Munshi, a Gujarati *litterateur*, the culture of Gujarat is greatly indebted to Gandhi's many literary pieces. 'As a specimen of literary art, the *Atmakatha* has its place among the best works in Gujarati prose.'[26] Through his style, Gandhi was able to combine two prevailing trends[27] in Gujarati literature by creating a powerful language of the people.

> His style is clear, lucid, precise, full of concentrated directness; it is stripped of rhetoric and the varied modes of sophistication, including the overload of Sanskrit forms which at this time had become an artificiality. While the quality of restraint in its full measure gives the writing an unerring sense of proportion, the literary element is always subordinated to the author's prime motive, which is to touch the living chord in the reader's heart.[28]

Although Gandhi began publishing articles in Gujarati as early as 1903 with the *Indian Opinion*, his popularity as a writer peaked only after 1930 when the public began to assimilate his thoughts in the context of the Satyagraha Movement. Dilip J. Thakore is of the opinion that his writings had created the Gandhian era in Gujarati literature.[29] It was in these years that they attained the height of their communicative power, such that the Government-suppressed *Navajivan*. The last issue was published on 10 January 1932.

Why were Gandhi's Gujarati writings so attractive to vast audiences all over Gujarat? Perhaps, his own question at a Gujarat Literary Conference may provide the clue:

> For whose sake are we going to have our literature? Not certainly for the great gentry of Ahmedabad. They can afford to engage literary men and have great libraries in their homes. But what about the poor man at the well who with unspeakable abuse is goading his bullocks to pull the big leather bucket?[30]

The secret of Gandhi's popularity was his self-effacing style that spoke to the lowliest readership. 'In simple easy Gujarati he addressed the people directly, argued with them, coaxed, rebuked them as one of themselves.'[31] He was a strong advocate of a type of art and literature that could speak to 'the millions'.[32] His ambition, he said, was 'to wipe every tear from every eye'.[33]

The Speaker

Whenever Gandhi spoke, his tone of voice, his intonation and his phrasing of words carried a strong inner conviction and sincerity of purpose. 'He was humble but also clear-cut and hard as a diamond, pleasant and soft spoken but inflexible and terribly earnest.'[34] In his public speeches he came across as a benign Guru, who, through reason and moral encouragement spoke in a steady, firm and deliberate manner as 'a symbol of uncompromising truth'.[35] He wanted to 'think audibly' and 'speak without reserve' like a pilgrim in conversation with fellow pilgrims on the road to Truth.[36]

He is commonly described as an extremely diffident person who lacked public speaking skills and whose public speeches were often described as failures.[37] A recent comparative study by Bligh and Robinson on Gandhi's use of rhetoric (in speaking and writing) demonstrates that he used 'significantly less charismatic language' than US social movement leaders and presidents.[38] His speech delivery style was not polished or dramatic. At times, he even had to appeal to his audience to stay quiet if they wanted to hear him speak.[39]

Yet, there was something about Gandhian encounters that kept audiences flocking to him. It was his presence and his personality that they had come to experience. Gandhi was a kind of speaker who developed an invisible rapport with his audiences, an intimate chemistry that a researcher's dry content analysis of his speeches is likely to miss. Claude Markovits, a French scholar on Gandhi, says it better:

> His speeches were in the nature of conversations with the crowd and were always didactic in intent. But as a teacher he did not lord over his pupils, in the manner of many Indian middle-class politicians. He knew how to meet his audience on equal terms and was not bothered with considerations of social etiquette. The magic of Gandhi's word operated through the special radiance of his personality rather than the specific content of his speeches, which were often freely interpreted by the audience. What mattered to them was to see him and hear him; the details of what he said were much less important.[40]

The Journalist

While in England as a student of law, Gandhi tried his hand at freelance journalism. He wrote on cultural issues, mainly with the intention of introducing vegetarianism and the festivals of India to the British. He was drawn to journalism because he recognised its importance for the transformation of society. Although untrained in journalism, his written output was prolific.

His first newspaper was *Indian Opinion* (1903–1914). It served as a mouthpiece for Indians in South Africa. It had a threefold aim: first, to make the grievances of the Indian community known to the Government, to the whites in South Africa, to England and to the people of India; second, to point out to Indians in South Africa their own shortcomings with a view to overcoming them; and third, to eliminate cultural and religious intolerance in the Indian community.[41] Initially, it had four sections, namely, Hindi, English, Gujarati and Tamil. Later, due to the lack of writers in Hindi and Tamil, these sections were discontinued. But the effects of this initiative began to be felt in places that mattered most. It was a powerful means to launch his ideas of *satyagraha*.

A year after his return to India, he was urged by well-wishers to take up the editorship of an English newspaper called *Young India*, earlier published by the management of the *Bombay Chronicle*. Gandhi accepted the job. In 1919 he also began editing a Gujarati monthly called *Navajivan*. This was the result of a desire to communicate to the non-English-speaking public. The monthly became so popular that he had to convert it to a weekly. Both *Navajivan* and *Young India* propagated themes that were strongly political. They promoted the *satyagraha* approach to combating political oppression. They were hugely successful during the Civil Disobedience Movement that climaxed in the Salt March. The Government frequently raided the editorial offices of these papers until they were forced to fold up in January 1932 with Gandhi's arrest.

But Gandhi's pen could not be stifled. A year after his arrest he began a new paper entitled *Harijan*[42] (1933–1948). It was 'solely devoted to the Harijan cause' and would 'scrupulously exclude all politics'[43].

His Journalistic Style, Tone and Attitude

A casual reading of Gandhi's writings will reveal the utter simplicity of his grammatical style. His choice of words and phrases are kept to the bare minimum. He uses small words, short sentences and simple grammar.[44] He often uses the active voice, which combined with his lucid thinking gives his writings a head-on impact. The content is focused and logically arranged. He comes straight to the point. Like an astute advocate, he presents the bare facts of a case and then proceeds to interpret and explain his point of view. Anyone reading Gandhi for the first time will be struck by his clarity, forthrightness and 'sober reasoning'.[45] John Haynes Holmes writes:

> Gandhi's literary achievement is more remarkable in view of the fact that he was never, in any sense of the phrase, a literary man [...] he had no special grace of style. Seldom, if ever, in his writings, did he rise to the heights of eloquence and beauty. Gandhiji's interests were never aesthetic, but rather pragmatic. He had no desire or ambition, no time, to be an artist. His one thought was of his own people, and his struggle to make them free. So he wrote with disciplined simplicity, seeking only to make himself clearly understood. The result was the one most important quality of literary act, namely, clarity [...]. [He] mastered his medium. He wrought a style which was perfect for his purpose of communication. To read his

writings is to think of content and not of style which means a triumph in the adaptation of means to ends.[46]

Notwithstanding the simplicity of style, Gandhi is profusely quoted by the media, from books on peace and non-violence to quotation-websites on the internet.[47] This phenomenal splurge of Gandhian citations need not be due to the quality of their content alone. The universal applicability of these quotations that often transcend geographic, religious and racial barriers is an equally important consideration. Many of Gandhi's sayings seem to speak for the whole of humanity. Conscious of this ingredient in his writings and discourses he once referred to its disadvantage: 'My language is aphoristic, it lacks precision. It is therefore open to several interpretations.'[48]

The tone of Gandhi's writings reflect his self-discipline. They are without ornate phraseology. They reflect an urgency to communicate value and meaning without ostentation. The passion for truth is presented courteously. There is a fundamental regard for the reader whoever he or she may be. His graciousness, transparency, humility, largesse and ability to forgive are as evident as his desire to be reasonable, simple and clear. Even in the most stressful circumstances, he does not allow his emotions to tarnish the content and manner of expression.

> To be true to my faith [in *satyagraha*], therefore, I may not write in anger or malice. I may not write idly. I may not write merely to excite passion. The reader can have no idea of the restraint I have to exercise from week to week in the choice of topics and my vocabulary. It is a training for me. It enables me to peep into myself and make discoveries of my weaknesses. Often my vanity dictates a smart expression or my anger a harsh adjective. It is a terrible ordeal but a fine exercise to remove these weeds.[49]

Gandhi's attitude to journalism was different from many of his contemporaries. It was for him a mission and not a mere profession. He was fully aware of the lure of the limelight and how journalists were often tempted to compromise the truth by favouring the wealthy and the powerful. For this reason, he was against the funding of newspapers through advertisements or sponsorships. His own journals did without them:

> In the very first month of *Indian Opinion*, I realized that the sole aim of journalism should be service. The newspaper press is a great power, but

just as an unchained torrent of water submerges whole countrysides and devastates crops, even so an uncontrolled pen serves but to destroy. If the control is from without, it proves more poisonous than want of control. It can be profitable only when exercised from within. If this line of reasoning is correct, how many of the journals in the world would stand the test? But who would stop those that are useless? And who should be the judge? The useful and the useless must, like good and evil generally, go on together, and man must make his choice.[50]

Journalism was an excellent means through which Gandhi interacted with the community he served. He grew in this interaction: 'the changes in the journal were indicative of changes in my life.'[51] His writings were exercises in being transparent to his readers. They mirrored his life. 'Week after week I poured out my soul in its columns, and expounded the principles and practice of *Satyagraha* as I understood it.'[52] It involved a strict discipline of daily introspection and reflection on problematic issues. The high quality of such journalism also educated the reader and solicited a response that demanded the same standards of excellence:

I cannot recall a word in those articles set down without thought or deliberation, or a word of conscious exaggeration, or anything merely to please. Indeed the journal became for me training in self-restraint, and for friends a medium through which to keep in touch with my thoughts. The critic found very little to which he could object. In fact, the tone of Indian Opinion compelled the critic to put a curb on his own pen.[53]

After Gandhi's death, Rajkumari Amrit Kaur, a close collaborator, gives us a glimpse of what it meant working shoulder to shoulder with Gandhi:

To those of us who had the privilege of working with Gandhiji every week when the *Harijan* was being edited by him, it seems strange to be writing for its columns without submitting the same to the searching gaze of that prince of journalists. The care and thought he bestowed on whatever he himself wrote, the eagle eye with which he vetted every word of what even a man like Mahadev Desai (his secretary) wrote, his insistence on right expression, on the adherence to truth where facts were concerned, on the necessity of not using one word more than necessary, his appreciation of good literary style, his ruthless weeding out of much or wholesale discarding of what one thought was good, all these are never to be forgotten lessons. But the remembrance of them makes one pause and wonder whether any one of our poor efforts can ever come up to the high standard of journalism which was Gandhiji's incomparable contribution to public life.[54]

The Letter-writer

Gandhi was one of the world's most prolific letter-writers.[55] His openness to all human beings, irrespective of race, nation, culture, religion, age, gender or intelligence, is evident from the diversity of individuals with whom he corresponded. His letters had wide-ranging purposes: they were logistical, pedagogical, political, philosophical and sometimes merely relational. They were addressed to relatives, friends, collaborators, Government officials and heads of State. His reach was universal. He wrote to Queen Victoria[56] and Adolph Hitler[57] just as he did to children and adolescents.[58] The length of the letters varied from one-sentence notes to pages of protracted paragraphs. The huge collection contains letters of friendship, letters of complaint, letters seeking forgiveness and reconciliation, letters that furthered dialogue between conflicting parties, letters that built bridges between enemies, letters that spoke the truth with firmness in situations camouflaged by lies.[59]

Rajendra Prasad[60] gives us an eye-witness account of Gandhi's dedication to letter-writing:

> He was a very regular correspondent. There was hardly a letter calling for a considered reply which he did not answer himself. Letters from individuals, dealing with their personal and private problems, constituted a considerable portion of his correspondence and his replies are valuable as guidance to others with similar problems. For a great period of his life, he did not take the assistance of any stenographer or typist, and used to write whatever he required in his own hand, and even when such assistance became unavoidable, he continued writing a great deal in his own hand. There were occasions when he became physically unable to write with the fingers of his right hand and, at a late stage in life, he learnt the art of writing with his left hand. He did the same thing with spinning.[61]

The content of his letters was never condescending, presumptuous, despairing or condemnatory. The economy and discretion in the use of words were impressive: no words were wasted and none were written in ways he would have to regret later. As in journalism so also in letter-writing, Gandhi grew through the letters he wrote, as they, in turn, invited his readers to maturity. Through their content, tone and style they contributed greatly to his widening reputation as a sincere human being who wanted only the good of his addressees. According to Bhattacharya:

> One piece of coloured thread runs, as it were, through all the letters, tying them together: they illuminate the simple humanity of this common–uncommon person, they are a-throb with his amazing warmth of heart, the secret of his endearing inner grace.[62]

As an editor of four newspapers, letter-writing was a sacred duty, an important way to stay in touch with his readership at all times.[63] It established a network of commitment to social change among truth-seekers across the subcontinent and the world:

> For me it became a means for the study of human nature in all its casts and shades, as I always aimed at establishing an intimate and clean bond between the editor and the readers. I was inundated with letters containing the outpourings of my correspondents' hearts. They were friendly, critical or bitter, according to the temper of the writer. It was a fine education for me to study, digest and answer all this correspondence. It was as though the community thought audibly through this correspondence with me. It made me thoroughly understand the responsibility of a journalist, and the hold I secured in this way over the community made the future campaign workable, dignified and irresistible.[64]

Not all letters were easy to write. There were those he had to draft and redraft many times over. But every attempt was an effort closer to letting the truth prevail in a manner that was gracious and honourable.[65] In delicate situations involving the culpability of persons, he dealt with *objective facts* and refrained from passing judgements. Such letters always concluded by allowing the guilty persons a chance to prove their innocence.[66]

The Communication Objective: Truth Not Consistency

Gandhi was an enigma to some of his contemporaries who found inconsistencies in his writings and speeches unnerving.[67] He himself admitted: 'Friends who know me have certified that I am as much a moderate as I am an extremist and as much a conservative as I am a radical. Hence, perhaps, it is my good fortune to have friends among these extreme types of men.'[68]

One instance of his inconsistencies was his unremitting critique of western civilisation with its dependence on machinery, and his readiness to use the same machinery when necessity demanded it. Or when he was critical of the railways in *Hind Swaraj*, yet he made extensive use of railway facilities to let his message of non-violence 'reach…as many ears and hearts as possible'.[69]

Fully aware of his inconsistencies, he refused to make consistency his dogma. 'Seeming consistency may be really sheer obstinacy.'[70] He did acknowledge, however, that underlying the inconsistencies there was a thread of consistency, a method in his madness, like nature that thrived on unity in diversity.[71] At the age of 64 he explained:

> I am not at all concerned with appearing to be consistent. In my pursuit after Truth, I have discarded many ideas and learnt many new things. Old as I am in age, I have no feeling that I have ceased to grow inwardly or that my growth will stop with the dissolution of the flesh. What I am concerned with is my readiness to obey the call of Truth, my God, from moment to moment....[72]

To readers who were puzzled by his apparent ambivalence he offered this guiding principle:

> [W]hen anybody finds any inconsistency between any two writings of mine, if he has still faith in my sanity, he would do well to choose the later of the two on the same subject.[73]

> My aim is not to be consistent with my previous statements on a given question, but to be consistent with truth as it may present itself to me at a given moment. The result has been that I have grown from truth to truth [...]. My words and deeds are dictated by prevailing conditions. There has been a gradual evolution in my environment and I react to it *as a Satyagrahi*.[74]

The real aim, Gandhi seems to say, is to be a true *satyagrahi* daily, that is, to be driven with a passion for truth in every situation that presents itself. There is no challenge in being preoccupied about consistency with one's past.

But how does one know what is true? Gandhi laments the fact that there are many who claim to have the truth without applying the conditions to arrive at it—almost as if people claim they are scientists without having cultivated the scientific temper. The 'conditions' to arrive at truth, Gandhi says, are the vows of honesty, *brahmacharya*, non-violence, poverty and non-possession.[75] The 'truthful temper' that sustains these conditions is humility and introspection: 'If you would swim on the bosom of the ocean of Truth, you must reduce yourself to a zero.'[76] *Satyagrahi*s will therefore pay keen attention to their voice of conscience which will teach them their limitations and spur them on to practise self-discipline. They will learn to seek truthfulness in what they communicate, in how they act in the company of others, but most of all, in the inner recesses of *thought* itself.

Communication as Conflict Resolution

Gandhi's adherence to truth in communication was best seen in the way he managed conflicts. The *CWMG* bears eloquent testimony to his total involvement in conflict resolution. The editors of the hundred-volume project confirm:

> The writings and speeches show remarkable self-restraint and moderation, strict conformity to truth and a desire to do full justice to the viewpoint of the opponent—characteristics which remained with him through life.[77]

This is indeed an exceptional feat for one who voluntarily entered the vortex of contentious and volatile situations whether in Johannesburg, Champaran, Kheda, Delhi, Dandi, Calcutta or Noakhali. Today, Gandhi's *satyagraha* has the distinction of being a scientific discipline that offers tested communication methodologies for conflict resolution.[78]

From start to finish, the underlying principle of Gandhian engagement with an opponent in a conflict is to keep the channels of communication open, to avoid intimidation and to remove all obstacles to dialogue. Such openness calls for, first, a well-planned strategy of social interaction and, second, a rigorous personal attitudinal discipline.[79] Mark Juergensmeyer lists ten personal communication attitudes based on Gandhian conflict resolution.[80] They are: do not avoid confrontation, stay open to communication and self criticism, find a resolution and hold fast to it, regard your opponent as a potential ally, make your tactics consistent with the goal, be flexible, be temperate, be proportionate, be disciplined and know when to quit.

Gandhi's method of communicating for communion and liberation is described by B.R. Nanda, the eminent Gandhian scholar, when he highlights the reasons that transformed Gandhi into the *Mahatma*:

> The truth is that in Gandhi's philosophy of *satyagraha*, the enemy was not regarded as an eternal enemy, but a potential friend. It was the duty of the *satyagrahi*s to reason with the adversary, to try to dispel his prejudices, to disarm his suspicions, to appeal to his dormant sense of humanity and justice, and, eventually to try to prick his conscience by inviting suffering at his hands. As Gandhi told a correspondent in April 1939, the *satyagrahi*'s object was 'not avoidance of all relationship with the opposing power', but 'the transformation of the relationship'. In South Africa, Gandhi had negotiated, fought, and finally reached an agreement with General Smuts. His parting gift to his chief antagonist was a pair of sandals which he had himself stitched. [...] In India, through a quarter of a century, Gandhi corresponded with all the Viceroys—Chelmsford, Reading, Irwin, Willingdon and Linlithgow—keeping his lines of communication open even while he engaged them in non-violent battle.[81]

Gandhi's character as a bridge-builder can be seen in the delicacy with which he answers questions put to him by the adolescent, Esther Faering. In the introduction to the book containing their letters,[82] the editor, Alice Barnes, considers Gandhi's replies as proof 'of the fine sensitiveness and generosity of his spirit; there is no attempt to influence the "child" to whom he writes, against the foreign rulers of India, no self-glorification or self-pity, no bitterness or rancour'.[83]

He boldly spoke out in defence of the non-violent nature of all his writings and speeches when he said: 'My life is a standing testimony against the libel.'[84]

A Gigantic People-to-People Communication Network

The written word was an important element in the *satyagraha* campaign as it expressed clearly the mind of the leader. Yet, Gandhi was aware that writing alone was insufficient to reach the illiterate millions scattered in remote towns and villages of the huge subcontinent. He began to create groups of volunteers to assist in the task of spreading the message by word of mouth and through folk media. He formulated a pledge[85] and made it obligatory for all volunteers. He challenged them to the high level of integrity essential for practising *satyagraha*. The pledges were first approved by the Congress and no Congress member had the right to change or water-down their implication. The volunteers had to wear *khadi*, they had to work for the eradication of untouchability, they had to be prepared to go to jail, they had to swear by non-violence and even die for the cause.[86]

Thousands responded. There were students and teachers who walked out of Government-run schools and colleges; there were lawyers and litigants who boycotted the courts; there were those who resigned from the army and the police in order to become Gandhi's volunteers.[87] The sole aim of this campaign was to extend and multiply the reach of the non-violent Non-cooperation Movement. From 1920 to 1927 the focus was on the struggle for *swaraj* through *swadeshi*; later it shifted to the wider constructive programme proposed by Gandhi and adopted by the Congress. The driving force behind this huge communication network was the zeal to 'make common cause' with the unreachable poor:

> The volunteers are called upon to enlist themselves in order to do village reconstruction work, and this village reconstruction work is nothing but the organization of the peasantry and workers upon an economic basis. We want to enter into the hearts of the peasants. We want to identify ourselves completely with the masses. We want to make their woes our own. We want to feel with them in everything in order to better the lot of those on whose toil we the people of the city are really living. We must therefore make common cause with the workers.[88]

Chakravarty, an eyewitness to this phenomenal empathy movement, shares his impressions:

> [Gandhi] left out no means and no technique to rouse the consciousness of the people and instil into them the imperative of their active participation in the movement [...]. The means to convey that message were often primitive, but no medium available at the time was left out. From traditional interpersonal means—including the travelling bards—the bauls of Bengal, for instance—to the educated student going

out on literacy-cum-swadeshi missions—the composing of patriotic songs and setting up choirs in villages, *mohallas* and *bustees*, to the immortal 'magic lantern', nothing was left out. It was a gigantic operation, sustained through the ups and downs of the freedom struggle, and later on followed by the handwritten posters and graffiti.[89]

Thanks to Gandhi's integrity and communication management skills, he was able to make his message reach places far beyond the influence of newspapers, telegraph, radio and rail–road transportation. The Freedom Movement was on a sound footing precisely because the villages were afire with the cry of *swaraj*.[90]

His Use of Mass Media and its International Repercussions

Gandhi's forceful critique of modern civilisation and its craze for machinery as a substitute for human labour did not deter him from making use of new technology to serve the cause of truth. He willingly used the media of mass communication to pass on his ideas of *satyagraha* and *ahimsa* to wider audiences, as is evident in his use of the printing press, cable and wireless telegraphy and the radio.

The very practice of *satyagraha* showed extreme media awareness. News coverage of the dramatic scenes of unilateral violence by the Government against submissive, non-violent *satyagrahis* made extremely sensational stories for worldwide consumption, and journalists flocked to cover these events. *Satyagraha* as a method of fighting colonial enslavement might not have had such an impact on the conscience of the world if it had not been followed up by heart-rending news reports and photographs.

It is amply evident that Gandhi was conscious of the importance of international news coverage for the success of *satyagraha*. He often declared that the Government's violent resistance to non-violent *satyagrahis* could not hold out for long. The British would have to surrender, at least for fear of being embarrassed before the world, if not for genuine sentiments of guilt or fear of anarchy. Gandhi therefore looked upon mass media as positive partners in the struggle for truth. His own choice to be a journalist in South Africa is proof of this conviction.

The *Newspaper* was the first channel through which he voiced his grievances about the treatment of Indians. Initially, he used the mainstream newspapers of South Africa, writing articles, letters to the editor and 'open letters' to the general public. He gave interviews to many papers sympathetic to his cause. But he soon realised that it was not enough to write sporadically and depend on the goodwill and hospitality of newspapers. For a sustained political campaign he needed an official and consistent mouthpiece. Furthermore, some of his writings, being daring critiques of Government policy and administration, were not accepted by mainstream newspapers. He therefore decided to begin printing and publishing on his own. That is how, in 1903, *Indian Opinion* was born—a paper that defined his identity as a truth-seeker and an advocate for justice.[91]

Gandhi also made extensive use of *cable and telegraph communication*. The first of his many cables noted in the *CWMG* was sent to the Colonial Secretary, Joseph Chamberlain from Durban on 7 May 1896. Gandhi requested him not to accept the Natal Franchise Bill that was discriminating against the Indian community. Gandhi sent similar cables to others, including Hunter and Dadabhai Naoroji.

By far the most notable moment of Indian history in the use of cable connections with Britain and the USA was around the time of the Salt March to Dandi. It would seem that Gandhi was well informed about the new developments in cable technology, and took full advantage of it for wider publicity. In 1929, a combined cable–radio company called the 'Imperial and International Communications' was created linking Britain to America and the British colonies. Exactly one year later, Gandhi organised the Salt March to Dandi, a plan he kept secret even from his closest collaborators.[92] It was a triumph of civil disobedience that was to affect the whole of India. Could it be that Gandhi had intentionally timed this event to attract an international audience? According to some passages in the *CWMG*, this hypothesis is probable. His classic message sent out by cable from Dandi on 5 April 1930, reveals his superb mastery of adapting content, language and style to the constraints of the new medium. It was crisp, cogent and poetic: 'I want world sympathy in this battle of Right against Might.'[93]

It is highly probable that Gandhi availed of the innovations in cable telecommunications to ensure international press coverage at the Dandi March for another reason. Years of interacting with the British

Government had made him aware of the extreme sensitivity of the English in maintaining a dignified image before the world. Exposing its unjust claim on India would be a perfect way to embarrass it and awaken the conscience of the world—especially after his previous attempts to convince it had failed. In a statement to the Associated Press he complimented the Government for its 'complete non-interference adopted throughout the march'. He admitted it came as a surprise and added:

> The only interpretation I can put upon this non-interference is that the British Government, powerful though it is, is sensitive to world opinion which will not tolerate repression of extreme political agitation which civil disobedience undoubtedly is.[94]

A month after he picked up a handful of salt at Dandi and broke the law, he was arrested and brought to Bombay where a reporter of *The Daily Telegraph* asked him for a message. He responded: 'Tell the people of America to study the issues closely and to judge them on their merits.'[95] Asked if he had any bitterness or ill-will towards anyone, he responded: 'None whatsoever; I had long expected to be arrested.'[96] His explicit message to America given to the correspondent of the Eastern News and Press Agency, New York, was:

> I know I have countless friends in America[97] who are in deep sympathy with this struggle but mere sympathy will avail me nothing. What is wanted is concrete expression of public opinion in favour of India's inherent right to independence and complete approval of the absolutely non-violent means adopted by the Indian National Congress. In all humility but in perfect truth I claim that if we attain our end through non-violent means India will have delivered a message for the world.[98]

Gandhi's plan to raise world opinion against British Imperialism seemed to work. In a matter of days, the struggle for *swaraj* was catapulted to the front pages of international journals. Gandhi was *Time* magazine's 1931 Man of the Year.[99] World opinion swung in his favour so effectively that the Government could not ignore the Indian question much longer. It organised three round table conferences from November 1930 to 1932 to resolve the Indian demand for independence. Indeed, the axe had been laid to the root, and the dismantling of international imperialism was only a matter of time.[100]

Gandhi's first radio broadcast was to America on the Columbia Broadcasting Service network. It was from Kingsley Hall, London, where he stayed as a guest of Muriel Lester during the second session of the Round Table Conference. Reporting on this event, Louis Fischer notes that before beginning his unprepared address, Gandhi said: 'Do I have to speak into that?' After the address was over, he remarked: 'Well that's over.' These words were heard by the listeners.[101]

Gandhi's second radio broadcast was on 12 November 1947, the feast of Diwali, and involved a visit to a Radio Broadcasting Studio. He humbly accepted to be tutored by the radio technicians who escorted him to the studio.[102] He spoke in clear Hindustani for 20 minutes, addressing 'My suffering brothers and sisters' of the Kurukshetra Camp.[103] This is how a report published after his death described the proceedings: a prayer meeting atmosphere was created in the studio which was specially fitted with the *takhposh*.[104] At first he was shy of the radio and it was after much persuasion that he agreed to broadcast from the studios of All India Radio. But the moment he reached the studio he seemed to own this impersonal instrument and said: 'This is a miraculous power. I see "shakti", the miraculous power of God.'[105]

Gandhi's Non-verbal Communication

Action was Gandhi's domain. He believed that what he did would endure over and above what he said or wrote.[106] Moreover, his spoken and written communication was accompanied by a rich variety of non-verbal symbolism that endeared him to the largely illiterate rural population that flocked to his open-air prayer meetings and conferences.[107] Some examples are his silence, fasting, clothing and physical presence.[108]

Silence (Mauna)

As Gandhi grew up, he was able to see the positive benefits of his initial shyness. One of them, we have already noted, was the economy of words. Another benefit was the ability to appreciate the value of silence:

> Experience has taught me that silence is part of the spiritual discipline of a votary of truth. Proneness to exaggerate, to suppress or modify the

truth, wittingly or unwittingly, is a natural weakness of man and silence is necessary in order to surmount it. A man of few words will rarely be thoughtless in his speech; he will measure every word. We find so many people impatient to talk. [...] All this talking can hardly be said to be of any benefit to the world. It is so much waste of time.[109]

This thirst for silence, motivated by his desire to shun idle talk and to be disciplined in the search for truth, urged him to take a vow of silence on every Monday of the week[110] as a 'means of introspection'.[111] He admitted that observing silence had become an essential part of his life. It did not demand much effort.

By introspection he meant entering into the consciousness of one's self through an 'attitude of silence [in which] the soul finds the path in a clearer light, and what is elusive and deceptive resolves itself into crystal clearness'.[112]

There were times when he would go on 'speech fasts'. They were occasions when he deliberately chose silence for longer periods—for a few days,[113] a whole week,[114] a whole month[115] and even indefinitely.[116] The motivations varied: to recoup his failing health; for physical and mental rest; in bereavement following the loss of loved ones or because of his sense of helplessness before events that were beyond his ability to control.[117]

Silence was a disposition that opened him to God, adored in the various names given by different religions. The encounter was not an occasion for asking favours but an act of sincere and childlike trust in Him who 'knows best what we need and what is beneficial for us'.[118]

Silence had a great qualitative effect on his communication. He believed that a votary of truth is someone who cultivates and values silence, both as an end and as a means: as an end the seeker encounters the truth in the depths of his or her being; as a means silence is the source from which the content and manner of speech and action emanate. Silence is therefore the treasure and the well-spring of a communication that inspires and uplifts. It is also the 'space' where meaning is discovered and formulated.[119] Gandhi cherished silence because he felt 'protected' within it, enabling him to work much better.[120]

But his silence also served another, although unintentional, purpose. His reputation as a 'saint' grew in public esteem. Many who encountered him experienced his silence as a reservoir of great moral strength. To the masses he was not merely a truth-seeker, he became the *symbol* of truth itself, and thousands flocked to have his *darshan*. Reflecting on

Gandhi's practice, Tagore commented, 'Does not such silence amount to a speech stronger than any uttered word?'[121]

Fasting (Upavas)

Gandhi stands out in world history as a leader who used fasting as a systematic means of non-violent, non-verbal persuasion. Allen H. Merriam, in an early study of Gandhian communication, says:

> Of all his techniques of symbolic action, the fast or hunger strike most typified Gandhi's character and temperament. Fasting afforded a method of influencing political policy and social attitudes by creating an emotional impact difficult to achieve through ordinary speech and negotiation. It also provided a source of spiritual renewal for a man dedicated to controlling his senses and desires.[122]

Gandhi also used fasting as a penance for a wrong done and to convert the heart of the offender.[123] It was often a symbol of self-purification, especially when embarking on a project of great magnitude and consequence.[124]

He undertook 15 fasts during his lifetime.[125] The motives ranged from the struggle for improved labour conditions for Ahmedabad mill workers to communal harmony between rival Hindu–Muslim factions. He developed guidelines for appropriate fasting: fasting must emanate from faith in God, must have a well-defined goal and must never be used for personal gain.[126] The fast would be effective only in a situation of mutual love, that is, when the sufferer holds a claim on the conscience of the adversary.[127] Fasting should only be resorted to against someone who is loved, not to extort rights from him but to reform him.[128] The supreme act of love meant sacrifice, because 'no man, if he is pure, has anything more precious to give than his life'.[129]

Nothing could be more powerful than Gandhi's fasts. No amount of words, either written or spoken could have produced the same dramatic effect that his fasts had on the psyche of the people. They sent ripples throughout India. His very last fast,[130] undertaken to stop the communal riots that were raging between Hindus and Muslims because of the creation of Pakistan, is a perfect example. As a result, the Indian Union Cabinet reversed its earlier decision and agreed to pay Pakistan its share of United India's cash balances amounting to Rs 55 crores or

£ 44 million.[131] It even changed the opinion of the sceptics: the Muslim League paid tributes to Gandhi despite 10 years of representing him as the enemy of Islam; the British press that had earlier deemed his fasts mere 'blackmailing antics' now considered his fast 'a power which may prove greater than the atom bomb'.[132] The Viceroy's press attaché, Alan Campbell-Johnson, who was present in Delhi during the time and who observed the immediate calm that prevailed as a public reaction to the fast wrote in his diary:

> You have to live in the vicinity of a Gandhi fast to understand its pull-ing power. The whole of Gandhi's life is a fascinating study in the art of influencing the masses, and judging by the success he has achieved in this mysterious domain, he must be accounted one of the greatest artists in leadership of all time. He has a genius for acting through symbols which all can understand.[133]

Knowing how the mass media attracts a wider readership by pub-lishing dramatic and heart-wrenching stories, Gandhi made use of self-suffering to tap into their potential for promoting socio-political change. The media attention put pressure on those responsible for the injustices and led to conversion:

> Experience has shown that mere appeal to the reason produces no effect upon those who have settled convictions. The eyes of their understand-ing are opened not by argument but by the suffering of the *satyagrahis*. The *satyagrahi* strives to reach the reason through the heart. The method of reaching the heart is to awaken public opinion. Public opinion for which one cares is a mightier force than that of gunpowder.[134]

The fast undertaken between 10 February and 3 March 1943 gives us a glimpse of the tremendous pressure exerted on the offenders to change their ways. Records of meetings of the British War Cabinet, made public as recently as January 2006, demonstrate the British Government's con-fusion in dealing with Gandhi's manner of peaceful opposition. Lord Linlithgow, the Viceroy of India in 1943, sent ministers a telegram stat-ing that he was 'strongly in favour of letting [Gandhi] starve to death'. Churchill was prepared to let Gandhi 'do as he likes'. But Lord Halifax (Irwin), Viceroy of India 1926–1931, told the Cabinet the day after Gandhi was arrested: 'Whatever the disadvantages of letting him out, his death in detention would be worse.' Sir Stafford Cripps, who in

March 1942 failed to negotiate a settlement with Gandhi so he would support the British War effort, said: 'He is such a semi-religious figure that his death in our hands would be a great blow and embarrassment to us.' Consequently, aware and fearful of the dangerous repercussions if Gandhi were to die in British custody, the Viceroy released Gandhi on 6 May 1944.[135]

Clothing

Before we take up a detailed analysis of Gandhi's use of clothing in the chapters that follow, a brief mention of it in the context of Gandhi's non-verbal communication is appropriate.

Gandhi's autobiography is replete with passages that highlight how his 'punctiliousness in dress persisted for years'.[136] In photographs of his childhood and adolescence, he is seen elegantly attired in his native Kathiawadi costume. While studying law in England and while practising it in South Africa, Gandhi wore the formal apparel common to British barristers. However, on reading John Ruskin's *Unto this Last*, he began to simplify his lifestyle. He initiated his *satyagraha* campaign by dressing in a white *kurta* and *dhoti* as a sign of mourning for the violence committed by the Government against the Indian indentured labourers of South Africa. On permanently returning to India he discarded Western fashion once and for all. He started the Swadeshi Movement by mobilising the Indian masses to boycott foreign cloth as it was the primary cause of India's poverty. He urged all his countrymen and women to burn foreign clothing and interpreted the bonfire as a purification rite for the sin of having cooperated with the British in the destruction of India's once flourishing weaving industry. In the place of foreign textiles, Gandhi began promoting home-spun *khadi*. He urged all Indians to dress in *khadi* alone and set the example himself. He soon learned that people in certain parts of India were too poor to afford *khadi*. In solidarity with them, and as an example that one's self-respect was of greater value in the fight for independence from foreign rule, Gandhi decided to reduce his conventional clothing to a mere waist-covering *dhoti* (or 'loin-cloth,' as it was commonly called by the British). It was this choice that immediately transformed him into an international icon.

Gandhi's sartorial evolution[137] revealed his intuitive grasp of the persuasive power of dress to touch the sensibilities of his audiences. His final clothing most represented the values he lived by: to be among the poorest of the poor, to hold no official government position, to live detached from material wealth, to sacrifice his family life for the birth of a nation and—most courageous of all—to lead with an appearance of ineptitude. This unique method of communicating had such tremendous impact on the masses that he was soon thrust into the front ranks of socio-political leadership. It earned him the reverence of the religiously inclined people of India who saw in him the saintly politician they had long been waiting for.

Physical Presence and Example

Gandhi was no armchair politician. He did not believe in being part of an elite club that spoke on behalf of the starving millions without first meeting them personally and feeling their pain. As soon as he returned from South Africa in 1915, he took Gopal Krishna Gokhale's advice to heart. He travelled around the country for a year, acquainting himself with the diversity of cultures, observing the harm caused by social barriers and getting to know the people's real needs. However, he went a step further than Gokhale's advice: he travelled third class! He chose to experience Indian life from the perspective of India's poorest.

This passion to be in the midst of the most vulnerable section of society was constant. Whenever he took up residence in Bombay or Delhi, he would stay in the *bhangi* quarters.[138] On his visit to London for the Round Table Conference he stayed in the East End, among the economically disadvantaged, in order to be 'among the same sort of people to whom I have given my life'.[139]

This way of being, this manner of seeing reality by imbibing knowledge through an active presence among the poorest, was at the root of his unique communication ability to transform India's liberation campaign from the preserve of an educated elite to a country-wide mass struggle. Historian Nanda confirms:

> The Mahatma's initial insights into the centrifugal factors in Indian society acquired in South Africa were further strengthened by his experience during the three decades when he stood at the centre of the political storms in the homeland. During these years he travelled from one end of the country to the other, and acquired at first hand a unique knowledge of the psychology of the Indian people. Not even the Buddha

and Sankaracharya could have known as intimately every nook and cranny of this country as Gandhi did.[140]

Merriam states that Gandhi spent one-third of the last 33 years of his life (from 1915 to his death in 1948) in travelling;[141] this amounts to approximately 10 years in close contact with people across the Indian subcontinent.[142] Jawaharlal Nehru once compared Gandhi's first impact on Indian politics and society to a 'hurricane'. His whirlwind tours deepened the national consciousness of millions of people who had hitherto been beyond the pale of politics.[143] During these journeys, Gandhi interacted with all through considerable verbal communication. At select destinations he gave speeches, conducted prayer meetings and held discussions. Yet his presence was more powerful than verbal assurances. His simplicity was a great lesson in solidarity. Many of the people looked upon him as an *avatar*—an incarnation of God. Throngs flocked to stations through which his train passed. Platforms of wayside stations were packed to overflowing with people sitting on station rooftops and on the footboard of his wagon, merely to get a *darshan*. To avoid accidents, his train had to be stopped at several places and the footboards cleared of people clinging on to them.[144] Once, during the 1933–34 trips to raise money for the cause of the Untouchables, he collected 350,000 Rupees from ordinary folk, and about 1.2 million people experienced his *darshan* and heard him speak in two weeks alone.[145]

To be nearer to people, Gandhi often went on foot. Walking was a fetish for him. It built up his physical stamina.[146] But health reasons aside, Gandhi gave long walks a symbolic meaning when he turned them into *padyatras* or walking pilgrimages. This was a non-violent way of manifesting determination, solidarity and struggle for justice. One such *padyatra* was in riot-stricken Noakhali and Tipperah in 1947. At the age of 77, he walked barefoot 116 miles through 47 villages, urging peace, and often quoting the Koran to his predominantly Muslim audiences.[147]

Gandhi's Charisma

The communicative power of Gandhi's presence worked like magic. Eyewitnesses and photographs reveal how people were awed by simply being in his presence. It was as though they were seeing a god.[148] Nehru gives us an idea of this 'feeling' in an exceptionally rich description of Gandhi's charisma:

> This little man of poor physique had something of steel in him, something rock-like which did not yield to physical powers, however great they might be. And in spite of his unimpressive features, his loin-cloth and bare body, there was a royalty and a kingliness in him which compelled a willing obeisance from others. Consciously and deliberately meek and humble, yet he was full of power and authority, and he knew it, and at times he was imperious enough, issuing commands which had to be obeyed. His calm, deep eyes would hold one and gently probe into the depths; his voice, clear and limpid, would purr its way into the heart and evoke an emotional response. Whether his audience consisted of one person or a thousand, the charm and magnetism of the man passed on to it, and each one had a feeling of communion with the speaker. This feeling had little to do with the mind, though the appeal to the mind was not wholly ignored. But mind and reason definitely had second place. This process of 'spell-binding' was not brought about by oratory or the hypnotism of silken phrases. The language was always simple and to the point and seldom was an unnecessary word used. It was the utter sincerity of the man and his personality that gripped; he gave the impression of tremendous inner reserves of power. [...] Every gesture had meaning and grace, without a false touch. There were no rough edges or sharp corners about him, no trace of vulgarity or commonness, in which unhappily our middle classes excel. Having found an inner peace, he radiated it to others and marched through life's tortuous ways with firm and undaunted step.[149]

This charismatic way of being among people was, by itself, a rich educational experience for those who opened their doors to receive him. His presence and example was a lesson in peace, equality and freedom. Thomas Weber, researcher on the Salt March, narrates:

> On the fourth day, at the lunch halt at the tobacco growing village of Dabhan, Gandhi was received with great enthusiasm. Perhaps the enthusiasm of the welcoming committee ebbed a little as Gandhi walked straight through the village, past the temple and the village square, to the untouchable quarters where he drew water from the well and bathed. The high-caste Hindus, who accompanied him were faced with a dilemma—mingle with the casteless or be rude to their honoured guest. And for someone like Gandhi to draw his own water, rather than have a servant do

it for him, was a small practical sermon on the kind of free India he envisaged. The salt march was the means, all the small examples set by himself and his marchers along the way were to be glimpses of the end.[150]

In a comparative study of social movement leaders and US presidents, Michelle Bligh examines whether charismatic rhetoric is a universal or culturally bound phenomenon. She concludes that Gandhi used 'significantly less charismatic language than either group, despite his overwhelming charismatic aura'. She thinks that the possible explanations for Gandhi's pervasive charismatic appeal lie in the fact that 'Gandhi's symbolic behaviors created a strong *contagion effect* among his followers'.[151] She refers to the theory of social contagion effect promoted by J.R. Meindl, which suggests that 'heightened levels of excitement and energy may create enough follower arousal to evoke charismatic attributions that are spread from follower to follower'[152]—a type of arousal that was a salient feature in the context of the tension between Indians fighting for their freedom and the British colonialists clinging on to their politics of Empire.

Gandhi as Message and Symbol

Gandhi's power of communication and strong charisma turned him into the embodiment of Indian independence. He spent his life communicating liberation but to the masses of Indian people he himself was the liberation he communicated. He epitomised the dream of *purna swaraj*. Nehru explains Gandhi's position within the Congress thus:

Congress was dominated by Gandhi and yet it was a peculiar domination, for the Congress was an active, rebellious, many-sided organization, full of variety of opinion, and not easily led this way or that. Often Gandhi toned down his position to meet the wishes of others, sometimes he accepted even an adverse decision. On some vital matters for him, he was adamant, and on more than one occasion there came a break between him and the Congress. But always *he was the symbol of India's independence* and militant nationalism, the unyielding opponent of all those who sought to enslave her, and it was as such a symbol that people gathered to him and accepted his lead, even though they disagreed with him on other matters. They did not always accept that lead when there was no active struggle going on, but when the struggle was inevitable that symbol became all important, and everything else was secondary.[153]

But his fame as the 'Mahatma' and his becoming the sacred icon in the eyes of millions had its own disadvantages. Unscrupulous persons desiring to profit from his prestige sought to publish spurious and pernicious ideas in his name. He had to warn his readers not to accept anything as written by him unless signed by him. But knowing that even his signature could be misused, he invited his readers to judge for themselves if published writings were truly his, even if they bore his name, on the basis of the trade mark principles that he lived for, namely, *satya* and *ahimsa*:

> My writings cannot be poisonous, they must be free from anger, for it is my special religious conviction that we cannot truly attain our goal by promoting ill will [...]. There can be no room for untruth in my writings, because it is my unshakable belief that there is no religion other than truth [...]. My writings cannot but be free from hatred towards any individual because it is my firm belief that it is love that sustains the earth.[154]

On 5 September 1947, in response to a journalist's plea to have a message for his readers, Gandhi wrote in Bengali: 'My life is my message.'[155] He was honestly saying that there was really no more messages to give, except his life. When one checks the chronology one cannot miss the meaning: the day when Gandhi made his boldest claim was wedged between 4 September, when he broke his fast at Calcutta after assurances by leaders of warring communal factions to stop the riots, and 6 September, the day he visited the leprosy hospital and spoke to staff and patients before he left for Delhi.[156] In decoding the message one recognises two of his important concerns: peace and a preferential care of the outcaste. He did not communicate what he did not practise first. In him the medium *was* the message.[157]

Is such synchrony in communication and life humanly possible? How could someone at the head of an extremely diversified and contentious population, someone who was constantly under media scrutiny, make such a claim to purity of intention in words and action, without losing his perseverance and peace?

At the end of this lengthy chapter on Gandhi's wide range of communication skills, it is fitting to let the Mahatma himself share his motivating secret:

What I want to achieve—what I have been striving and pining to achieve these thirty years—is self-realization, to see God face to face, to attain *Moksha*. I live and move and have my being in pursuit of this goal. All that I do by way of speaking and writing, and all my ventures in the political field, are directed to this same end.[158]

Notes

1. M.K. Gandhi, *The Collected Works of Mahatma Gandhi*, vol. 33 (New Delhi: Publications Division, Government of India, 1994), 144. (Henceforth *CWMG*).
2. Cf. Nikhil Chakravarty, 'Mahatma Gandhi: The Great Communicator', *Gandhi Marg* (1995), 16 (4): 89–91.
3. The French Revolution (1789–1799) was initiated in Paris by a few thousands. The Russian Revolutions (1905, 1917, 1918–1922) were caused by a series of peasant unrests and were led by a small band of determined and organised militant revolutionaries headed by Lenin and the Bolsheviks who captured power when the Czarist system collapsed during World War I. The Chinese Cultural Revolution (1966–1968) was led by some thousand people under the dynamic Mao Zedong, who roused the peasantry through an armed march across the countryside. Cf. *ibid.*
4. *Satyagraha* means 'Force of Truth'.
5. Krishnalal Shridharani, *War without Violence: A Study of Gandhi's Method and its Accomplishments* (New York: Brace Harcourt, 1939), 3. This work was to have a profound impact on the civil rights movement led by Martin Luther King Jr.
6. Cf. B.R. Nanda, *In Search of Gandhi, Essays and Reflections* (New Delhi: Oxford University Press, 2002), 145. Taken from the diary of Sir Thomas Jones (details not stated).
7. Cf. *CWMG*, vol. 89, 529.
8. M.K. Gandhi, *Hind Swaraj and Other Writings*, ed., Anthony J. Parel, (New Delhi: Foundation Books, 2004), 107.
9. Albert Einstein's celebrated words on Gandhi: 'Generations to come will scarce believe that such a one as this ever in flesh and blood walked upon this earth.' D.G. Tendulkar, *Mahatma*, vol. 6, 286 quoted in Bhabani Bhattacharaya, *Gandhi the Writer* (New Delhi: National Book Trust, 1969/2002), 287.
10. Johanna McGeary, 'Mohandas Gandhi', *Time* (31 December 1999), 91. Praise for Gandhi's communication ability has been acknowledged in research articles and books. Some examples are: S.N. Bhattacharyya, *Mahatma Gandhi the Journalist*, 1965; Bhabani Bhattacharya, *Gandhi the Writer*, 1969; Allen Merriam, 'Symbolic Action in India: Gandhi's Nonverbal Persuasion', *Quarterly Journal of Speech*, 1975; K.J. Singh, 'Gandhi and Mao as mass communicators', *Journal of Communication*, 1979; Keval Kumar, 'Gandhi's Ideological Clothing', *Media Development*, 1984; Nikhil Chakravarty, 'Mahatma Gandhi: The Great Communicator', *Gandhi Marg*, 1995; Emma Tarlo, *Clothing Matters—Dress and Identity in India*, 1996; Bharati Narasimhan, ed., *Making of a Great Communicator—Gandhi*, 1997.

11. Sarojini Naidu jokingly called Gandhi 'Mickey Mouse'. Cf. Jyotsna Kamat, 'Sarojini Naidu', http://www.kamat.com/kalranga/freedom/naidu.htm (3 January 2008).

12. M.K. Gandhi, *An Autobiography* or *The Story of My Experiments with Truth* (Ahmedabad: Navajivan, 1927/2005), 57. The paragraph that follows deals with Gandhi's ability to view his shyness no longer as an impediment but as an advantage.

13. *Ibid.*, 58.

14. Bharati Narasimhan, ed., *Making of a Great Communicator–Gandhi* (New Delhi: National Media Centre, 1997), iv.

15. 'Foreword', *CWMG*, vol. 1, ix.

16. 'Preface', *CWMG*, vol. 1, xiii.

17. Mahadev Desai was his devoted secretary for over 25 years. Some of those who compiled books from Gandhi's articles are Anand T. Hingorani, H.M. Vyas and Raavindra Kelekar.

18. 'Homage', *CWMG*, vol. 1, v.

19. Cf. *CWMG*, vol. 14, 120.

20. *CWMG*, vol. 13, 320.

21. *CWMG*, vol. 13, 321.

22. Indian historian Sunil Khilnani has observed, 'English made the empire, but [Gandhi and Jawaharlal Nehru] showed how it could be used to unmake it—how the language could be a tool of insubordination and, ultimately, freedom.' Chandrahas Choudhury, '*The Middle Stage*', http://middlestage.blogspot.com/2007/07/on-rajmohan-gandhis-biography-of.html (6 September 2007).

23. Cf. *CWMG*, vol. 48, 351. At the Plenary Session, Sir Hubert Carr shared his positive outlook on the Conference in contrast to many negative opinions that had been expressed by other speakers. He believed it enlightened the English people about the needs of Indians and made them understand Gandhi better. 'Without their work Mahatma Gandhi might have remained for many people in this country a more or less mythical figure, making salt in forbidden places or weaving all kinds of yarns.' Gandhi quickly added: 'You mean *spinning* all kinds of yarns.' Note Gandhi's correct idiomatic usage and his ability to enjoy the intended pun.

24. Edward John Thompson (1886–1946) was a novelist, poet, journalist and historian of India. See his biography by Mary Lago, *India's Prisoner* (Columbia MO: University of Missouri Press, 2001).

25. Edward Thompson, 'Gandhi: A Character Study', in *Mahatma Gandhi—Essays and Reflections*, ed., S. Radhakrishnan (Mumbai: Jaico Publishing House, 2004), 290–91.

26. K.M. Munshi, *Gujarati and its Literature* (Bombay: Longmans Green & Co., 1935), 312, cited in Bhattacharya, *Gandhi the Writer*, 91.

27. Gujarati literature had two trends, the Gujarati style and the Saurashtra style. Both were pedantic, having literary flourishes and liberal borrowings from Sanskrit or Persian.

28. K.M. Munshi, *Gujarati and Its Literature* (Bombay: Longmans Green & Co., 1935), 312, cited in Bhattacharya, *Gandhi the Writer*, 91.

29. Cf. Dilip J. Thakore, *Gandhian Era in Gujarati Literature* (Rajkot: Jyoti Prakashan, Mandir, 1955), 8.

30. *CWMG*, vol. 63, 413.

31. Preface, *CWMG*, vol. 16, ix.

32. The expression, 'the millions', was often used by Gandhi to refer to the poor and illiterate masses dispersed throughout the Indian subcontinent.

33. Jawaharlal Nehru, *The Discovery of India* (New Delhi: Penguin Books, 2004), 399.

34. Jawaharlal Nehru, *An Autobiography* (New Delhi: Penguin Books, 2004), 51.

35. Nehru, *Discovery of India*, 393.

36. Cf. *CWMG*, vol. 13, 212.

37. Cf. Susanna Hoeber Rudolph and Lloyd I. Rudolph, *Gandhi: The Traditional Roots of Charisma* (Chicago: University of Chicago Press, 1983), cited by M.C. Bligh and J.L. Robinson, 'Different Routes to Charisma and Taking the Road Less Travelled: An Analysis of Gandhi's Rhetorical Leadership', *Cross-Cultural Leadership and Management Studies* 1 (2004): 109–25, web version: www.cgu.edu/include/flmspr04.pdf (24 May 2005).

38. Cf. Bligh and Robinson, *Different Routes to Charisma*, 109–125.

39. Cf. *CWMG*, vol. 43, 27. 'I know that my voice will not reach you all. In the first place it does not have the power it once had. And then no man's voice can be heard by such a large crowd. I must be content if a few of these men and women can hear me. More people will be able to hear if those that cannot hear will be quiet and wait till their neighbours can give them a report of the speech.'

40. Claude Markovits, *The Un-Gandhian Gandhi, The Life and Afterlife of the Mahatma* (Delhi: Permanent Black, 2004), 140.

41. Gandhi, *Indian Opinion*, 28 April 1906; quoted in Bharati Narasimhan, ed., *Making of a Great Communicator—Gandhi* (Delhi: National Media Centre, 1997), 272–73.

42. *Harijan* began on 11 February 1933.

43. Sailendra Nath Bhattacharyya, *Mahatma Gandhi the Journalist* (Bombay: Asia Publishing House, 1965), 55.

44. A content analysis done on a sample of Gandhi's writings revealed that the use of difficult words (that is, those with more than three syllables) was minimal. The average number of syllables per word amounts to 1.49, out of a total average of 729.41 words per article. The number of different words used in an article (with an average 729 words) is 314.39. 'There is an almost perfect correlation between the total number of words and the number of different words [...] a clear indicator to say that despite the fact that simple words were used in the articles under consideration, the vocabulary of the author was in no way limited.' Ralin de Souza, 'Gandhian Style of Journalism' (dissertation for the Master's Degree in Communications, Salesian University, 2007), 87–90.

45. 'Sober reasoning' was a journalistic trait Gandhi consciously strove to cultivate. He lamented that many journalists were not sufficiently prepared for their responsible task: 'Too often in our journals as in others do we get fiction instead of fact and declamation in place of sober reasoning.' Gandhi, *Message for the Independent*, 30 January 1919, cited by Narasimhan, *Making of a Great Communicator*, 182.

46. Cited by Sunil Sharma, ed., *Journalist Gandhi—Selected Writings of Gandhi* (Bombay: Gandhi Book Centre, 1960), 11–12. John H. Holmes (1879–1964) was the founder and chairman of the board of the American Civil Liberties Union and the founder of the India League of America that fought to increase the support for Indian demands for independence from British rule.

47. A Google search of the words, 'Gandhi quotes', runs into 345,000 entries with some sites dedicated exclusively to his aphorisms (14 January 2008).

48. *CWMG*, vol. 53, 485.

49. *CWMG*, vol. 27, 322. To put this statement in context, it is worth looking at the preceding lines that explain Gandhi's mission as a journalist: 'I have taken up journalism not for its sake but merely as an aid to what I have conceived to be my mission in life. My mission is to teach by example and precept, under severe restraint, the use of the matchless weapon of *satyagraha* which is a direct corollary of non-violence and truth. I am anxious, indeed I am impatient, to demonstrate that there is no remedy for the many ills of life save that of non-violence. It is a solvent strong enough to melt the stoniest heart. To be true to my faith, therefore...'

50. M.K. Gandhi, *Autobiography*, 263–64.

51. *Ibid.*, 263.

52. *Ibid.*

53. *Ibid.*

54. *Harijan*, 11 April 1948; cited in Bhattacharya, *Gandhi the Writer*, 202–03.

55. *Ibid.*, p. 295.

56. His first correspondence with the Queen was an 'Address to Queen Victoria', (prior to 3 June 1897, GOI, *CWMG*, vol. 2, 317).

57. Gandhi wrote his first letter to Adolph Hitler on 23 July 1939 (*CWMG*, vol. 70, 20–21) and the second letter on 24 December 1940 (*CWMG*, vol. 70, 253–55).

58. As an example see *CWMG*, vol. 13, 327. See also 'Correspondence between Esther Faering and Mahatma Gandhi 1917' in the website of *The Danish Peace Academy*, http://www.fredsakademiet.dk/library/nordic/child.htm (8 February 2008).

59. One need only look at the letters of Gandhi to Lord Irwin, Hitler and Churchill to recognise the forthright manner in which he expressed his point of view while respecting the addressee's freedom to disagree.

60. Rajendra Prasad (1884–1963) was the first President of the Republic of India. He was one of the chief volunteers in Gandhi's Champaran *Satyagraha* (1918–1919).

61. *CWMG*, vol. 1, vi.

62. Bhattacharya, *Gandhi the Writer*, 295.

63. 'Many correspondents probably feel disappointed because their letters do not receive full justice. Readers of *Navajivan* know that great care is being exercised about the matter published in it. Therefore, letters from correspondents are utilized only when space is available...' *CWMG*, vol. 19, 296.

64. Gandhi, *Autobiography*, 263.

65. See for example, his letter to the daughter of the landlady who had ambitions of flirting with him. At the end of the letter he adds: 'Let the reader know that I could not have written such a letter in a moment. I must have drafted and redrafted it many times over. But it lifted a burden that was weighing me down.' M.K Gandhi, *Autobiography*, 61.

66. See three sample letters in the Appendix, 'Gandhi's Letter-Writing in Conflict', 142–43.
67. See Annie Besant's strong critique of Gandhi's writings in Natrajan, *History of the Press* (details not mentioned), quoted by Narasimhan, *Making of a Great Communicator*, vi.
68. R.K. Prabhu and U.R. Rao, *The Mind of Mahatma Gandhi* (Ahmedabad: Navajivan Publishing House, 1945/2002), 37 (Henceforth *MMG*).
69. *CWMG*, vol. 33, 144. The complete citation heads this chapter.
70. R.K. Prabhu and U.R. Rao, *MMG*, 36. He endorsed a quotation from Emerson: 'Foolish consistency is the hobgoblin of little minds.'
71. *Ibid.*, 37.
72. *Ibid.*, 37–38.
73. Gandhi, *Harijan*, 29 April 1933, 2.
74. 'Foreword', in *CWMG*, vol. 90, v (italics mine).
75. *CWMG*, vol. 48, 405–06.
76. *Ibid.*, 406.
77. 'Preface to the First Volume', in *CWMG*, vol. 1, xix.
78. I refer to just three of the many examples of Gandhi-inspired conflict resolution initiatives: the Shanti Sena—1957–1975 [See Thomas Weber, *Syracuse Studies on Peace & Conflict Resolution* (New York: Syracuse University Press, 1995)]; the Transcend University of Johan Galtung (www.transcend.org/); and the Conflict Resolution Education of Juergensmeyer [Mark Juergensmeyer, *Gandhi's Way: A Handbook of Conflict Resolution* (Berkeley: University of California Press, 2005)].
79. See. articles by Arnold Naess, Robert Bode and Allen Merriam in the bibliography.
80. Cf. Mark Juergensmeyer, *Gandhi's Way*, 63–64.
81. Nanda, *In Search of Gandhi*, 141.
82. Alice Barnes, ed., *My Dear Child, Letters from M.K. Gandhi to Esther Faering* (Ahmedabad: Navajivan Publishing House, 1956). See also *The Danish Peace Academy*, http://www.fredsakademiet.dk/library/nordic/child.htm (9 February 2008).
83. Alice Barnes, ed., *My Dear Child*, Introduction, website quoted above.
84. *CWMG*, vol. 26, 333.
85. Cf. *CWMG*, vol. 22, 100–01. No one was to be accepted as a volunteer who did not sign the eight-point pledge.
86. Requisite qualifications and duties of volunteers are described in detail in M.K. Gandhi, *Village Swaraj*, ed., H.M. Vyas (Ahmedabad: Navajivan Trust, 2002), 217–18.
87. Cf. B.R. Nanda, *Mahatma Gandhi: A Biography* (New Delhi: Oxford University Press, 2002), 204.
88. *CWMG*, vol. 38, 311–12.
89. Nikhil Chakravarty, 'Mahatma Gandhi: The Great Communicator', *Gandhi Marg* (1995): 393.
90. Cf. Janardan Pandey, ed., *Gandhi and Voluntary Organizations* (Bhagalpur: M.D. Publications, 1998).
91. '*Satyagraha* would probably have been impossible without *Indian Opinion*. The readers looked forward to it for a trustworthy account of the Satyagraha campaign

as also of the real condition of Indians in South Africa.' Gandhi, *Autobiography*, 263.

92. Nehru, *An Autobiography*, 221.

93. *CWMG*, vol. 43, 180. Other examples during the period 5 to 9 April 1930 that testify to his awareness of international interest in the happenings at Dandi—an unlikely corner of India for an international stage—may be found in, *CWMG*, vol. 43: 'Statement to Associated Press,' 179–80; 'Message to America', 180; 'Interview to Free Press of India', 199; 'Statement to the Press', 205; 'Message to the Nation', 214.

94. *CWMG*, vol. 43, 179. 'World Opinion' was represented by the presence of reporters from important international news agencies during the march and at Dandi.

95. *CWMG*, vol. 43, 400.

96. *Ibid*.

97. Some of his friends were Indian settlers in the USA. Cf., Francis C. Assisi, 'How South Asian Americans Breached the Great White Wall,' in *Sikhs, Swamis, Students, and Spies: The India Lobby in the United States, 1900–1946*, ed., Harold Gould (California: Sage Publications, 2006), web version *Indolink*: http://www.indolink.com/printArticleS.php?id=100906114336 (21 November 2006). Cf. *The Hindu*: 'FDR [Roosevelt] was pressing Churchill that he should do something for India and her demand for freedom. So Churchill knew he had to make some kind of gesture to the Americans to get them off his back [He allowed the Cripps mission to take its course with the hope that it would fail],' http://www.thehindu.com/thehindu/mag/2003/11/30/stories/2003113000310500.htm (24 December 2007).

98. The 'Message to America' was given on 5 April 1930 but was published in the Government-controlled *Bombay Chronicle* two days later. *CWMG*, vol. 43, p. 180.

99. Gandhi was on the cover of *Time Magazine* twice in the span of nine months: on 31 March 1930 for the Dandi March (the cover article was entitled 'Pinch of Salt'), and on 5 January 1931 as 'Man of the Year'.

100. Thanks to Gandhi, 'two-thirds of (the British Empire) got independent overnight'—the words of London Mayor Ken Livingstone. Cf. 'Mayor Wants to See Gandhi Statue,' *BBC News*, 20 September 2007 (web page cited earlier).

101. Cf. *CWMG*, vol. 48, 8.

102. He told them: 'You can regard me as an almost uncivilized person and tutor me about my talk'. *CWMG*, vol. 90, 15.

103. Over two lakh of refugees had arrived at Kurukshetra and more were pouring in. 'The moment the news came to me, I longed to be with you but I could not […] Seth Ghanshyamdas Birla suggested that I should broadcast a message to you and hence this talk'. *CWMG*, vol. 90, 15.

104. A *takhposh* is a low wooden settee which was daily used by him for addressing participants at the prayer meetings held at Birla House, Delhi.

105. V.S. Gupta, 'Mahatma Gandhi and Mass Media,' *Employment News* 26 (September–October 2001), web version: http://www.mkgandhi.org/mass_media.htm (10 December 2007). It is worth mentioning that a three-month clandestine radio called the Congress Radio operated during the Quit India movement of 1942 when Gandhi and most national leaders were in jail. Cf. Owen Williamson,

'The Mahatma's Hams,' World Radio, http://www.wr6wr.com/newSite/articles/features/mahatmashams.html (30 September 2007).

106. Cf. Gandhi, *Harijan*, 1 May 1947, 93; *MMG*, 41.

107. *Darshan* involves 'seeing' a deity or saint and thereby receiving blessings; *mahaatma* literally means 'great soul'.

108. Other symbolic actions worth considering are imprisonment, the spinning wheel and the march. For a detailed study of the symbolic actions employed in the Satyagraha Movement see, Krishnalal Shridharani, *War without Violence: A Study of Gandhi's Method and its Accomplishments* (New York: Brace Harcourt, 1939).

109. Gandhi, *Autobiography*, 58.

110. Gandhi is reported to have maintained week-long silences from 13 September 1922. However, the 'Chronology' of the *CWMG* states that he 'resumed practice of observing silence every Monday' on 17 March 1924. The exact date when he began maintaining the Monday silence is not ascertainable.

111. *CWMG*, vol. 89, 362.

112. An extremely popular quotation on the internet attributed to Gandhi is: 'In the attitude of silence the soul finds the path in a clearer light, and what is elusive and deceptive resolves itself into crystal clearness.' I have not been able to trace the original source (15 November 2006).

113. He observed silence for 91 hours commencing from 20 August 1942.

114. He observed silence from September 13 and again from 20 September 1922.

115. He observed silence from March 22 to 19 April 1935.

116. He observed silence 24 May 1940 onwards.

117. Here are three examples: on 13 September 1922 while in Yerwada jail; on 7 May 1928, the day Maganlal Gandhi died; on 20 August 1942 to mourn the death of his loyal secretary, Mahadev Desai, and to disapprove the Chimur riots of 16 August 1942. Cf. K.P. Goswami, *M. Gandhi—A Chronology* (Delhi: Publications Division, Government of India, 1971).

118. *CWMG*, vol. 89, 362.

119. Cf. Alfred Korzybski, *Science and Sanity* (Connecticut: International Non-Aristotelian Library Publishers, 1958). Korzybski (1879–1950) is the founder of General Semantics that states that 'the word is not the thing it represents,' which is why the non-verbal experiencing of our inner and outer environments needs to be emphasised. For this experience one must be 'outwardly and inwardly silent'. It is interesting to note that Korzybski arrived at these conclusions at the same time that Gandhi was discovering through silence his inner and outer worlds in the pursuit of Truth.

120. Cf. D.G. Tendulkar, *Mahatma*, (Delhi: Publications Division, 1951–1954/1960), 359.

121. Quoted in R.K. Prabhu and R. Kelekar, eds., *Truth Called Them Differently— Tagore Gandhi Controversy* (Ahmedabad: Navajivan, 1961), 94.

122. Allen H. Merriam, 'Symbolic Action in India: Gandhi's Nonverbal Persuasion', *Quarterly Journal of Speech*, 61(1975): 290.

123. See the incident regarding a 'moral fall' of two inmates at Phoenix that triggered Gandhi's decision to fast: Gandhi, *Autobiography*, 314–15.

124. Gandhi called upon the whole of India to fast for 24 hours 'as an act of self-purification' before embarking on a general *hartal* on 6 April 1919. Gandhi, *Autobiography*, 423.

125. See Gandhi's fasts in India and two examples of their effect, *ibid.*, Appendix, 1 and 2, 137–41.

126. Cf. Merriam, *Symbolic Action in India*, 293.

127. *Ibid.*

128. *CWMG*, vol. 23, 420.

129. Words of Gandhi cited in Krishna Kripalani, *Gandhi: A Life* (New Delhi: National Book Trust, 1982), 189.

130. In a letter to his disciple Miraben, he called his last fast for communal amity his 'greatest fast'. He began it on 13 January 1948 and ended it after five days.

131. Nanda, *The Making of a Nation*, 310. Privately Gandhi had asked Mountbatten what he personally thought of the Indian Cabinet's decision to withhold the payment to Pakistan. Mountbatten replied that such withholding would be the 'first dishonourable act' of the Indian Government. Cf. Kripalani, *Gandhi: A Life*, 187.

132. Cf. Kripalani, *Gandhi: A Life*, 189 and Nanda, *Mahatma*, 510.

133. Kripalani, *Gandhi: A Life*, 188.

134. *CWMG*, vol. 26, 327.

135. Sir Norman Brook in his own style of shorthand provides the first detailed insight into what was said during debates on crucial issues during the War Cabinet. Cf. 'Demands to let Gandhi die on hunger strike', *Timesonline*, 1 January 2006, http://www.timesonline.co.uk/article/0,,2087-1965609,00.html (5 January 2006).

136. Nehru, *An Autobiography*, 48.

137. See Peter Gonsalves, 'Half-naked Fakir: The Story of Gandhi's Personal Search for Sartorial Integrity', *Gandhi Marg*, 31(1): 5–30.

138. *Bhangi*s are the lowest among the Untouchables. To them is assigned the task of cleaning toilets and removing excreta wherever found. See Gandhi's note on living with *bhangi*s in *CWMG*, vol. 83, 317.

139. He accepted the invitation of his friend Muriel Lester to stay in the East End. So as not to inconvenience his fellow delegates and colleagues, however, he agreed to have an office at Knightsbridge. He mixed with the neighbourhood and made friends with the children. 'Here I am, doing the real round table work, getting to know the people of England.' Nanda, *Mahatma Gandhi*, 311–12.

140. Nanda, *In search of Gandhi*, 145. See also Nehru's comment on Gandhi's extensive travel: Nehru, *An Autobiography*, 202.

141. Cf. Merriam, *Symbolic Action in India*, 297.

142. For a sample of Gandhi's journeys during a 10-year period, see Appendix, 'A Ten-Year Sample of Gandhi's Journeys (1915–1925)', 141.

143. Cf. Nanda, *In Search of Gandhi*, 145.

144. Cf. Tendulkar, *Mahatma*, 347–406.

145. *Ibid.*

146. Before the Salt March to Dandi, a distance of 241 miles, he calculated the possible health hazards and arrived at the conclusion that it would be 'child's play'. He was 61. *CWMG*, vol. 43, p. 169.

147. Cf. Merriam, *Symbolic Action in India*, 298.

148. Cf. Tendulkar, *Mahatma*, vol. 7, 310.
149. Nehru, *An Autobiography*, 137–38.
150. Thomas Weber, 'Gandhi's Salt March as Living Sermon', *Gandhi Marg,* 22(4): 423.
151. Cf. Bligh and Robinson, *Different Routes to Charisma* (web page cited earlier).
152. *Ibid.*
153. Nehru, *The Discovery of India*, 399–400.
154. Prabhu and Rao, *MMG*, 40.
155. Written in Bengali on 7 September 1947. See Peter Rühe, *Gandhi: A Photo Biography* (London: Phaidon Press, 2001), 1.
156. Cf. *CWMG*, vol. 89, 529. The journalist was from the *Shanti Sena Dal.* The photograph of the original script in Bengali is in Rühe, *Gandhi*, 1. The date mentioned is 7 September 1947.
157. Gandhi continues to be a symbol for the whole world. As recently as 15 June 2007, the UN General Assembly declared his birthday, 2 October, as the International Day of Non-Violence. Cf. 'Mahatma Gandhi's Teachings Reflect UN Ideals Says UN Chief,' *United Nations Radio News Service*, 2 October 2007: http://www.un.org/radio/news/html/13506.html (12 October 2007). In India, Gandhi still cannot be ignored: 'That, 60 years after his death, the extremists of left and right still need to vilify him is in itself a considerable tribute to the relevance of his thought. So, in a somewhat different way, is the need for mainstream politicians to garland portraits of Gandhi even if their practice is at odds with the man they profess to honour.' Ramachandra Guha, 'A Father Betrayed', *The Guardian*, 14 August 2007, http://www.guardian.co.uk/india/story/0,,2148286,00.html (25 September 2007).
158. Gandhi, *Autobiography*, xii. The word *moksha* literally means freedom from the cycle of birth and death. The nearest English equivalent is 'salvation'.

2

Barthes: A Gandhian Fashion System

We now know…that a text is not a line of words releasing a single 'theological' meaning (the 'message' of an Author–God) but a multidimensional space in which a variety of writings, none of them original, blend and clash. The text is a tissue of quotations drawn from the innumerable centres of culture.[1]

Roland Barthes

Semiology or semiotics is the science of signs and symbols, of how they work and the way we use them.[2] In this chapter we will apply semiology to Gandhi's reconstruction of socio-political sartorial identity. We will be guided by the theory of Roland Barthes (1915–1980), a French cultural analyst, structuralist and semiotician.

Following the linguistic, structuralist tradition of Ferdinand de Saussure (1857–1913), Barthes looked at cultural phenomena as language systems. Saussure's central insight is the arbitrary nature of signs in language. Barthes applies Saussure's theory beyond language to phenomena as banal as novels, advertisements, photography, fashion, films, music and even notions of the self, of history and of nature. Barthes thus shifted Saussure's emphasis from the semiotics *of* language to the exploration of semiotics *as* language, thus enabling it to probe and unravel significance in all media of human communication as—he once admitted: 'What has fascinated me all my life is the way people make their world intelligible.'[3]

In this chapter I present some key insights of Barthes's semiotics of clothing as elaborated in his book, *Système de la Mode* (The Fashion System).[4] The book deals with the methodological approaches to the question of 'fashion' as described by fashion literature. My particular interest is the application of Barthes's methodology to the role of clothing in colonial life in India during the pre-Gandhian and Gandhian periods. I wish to draw inspiration from essential portions of Barthes's dense and detailed analysis of the written system of fashion. I might seem to be using only a part of Barthes's elaborate thesis on the 'written garment' for my purpose, but I do so in fidelity to his general semiotic framework, a part of which I shall elaborate here. Putting Barthes's theory to the test, even in a context as remote as the end of colonial rule in the Indian subcontinent is, I believe, an exciting way to understand his first work on fashion, described modestly by him as 'the beliefs, the temptations and the trials of an apprenticeship'.[5]

Signs and Sign Systems

Barthes's semiotics is built on the foundations of the Saussurean model of the linguistic sign. Every sign is a composite of a signifier and a signified. The *signifier* is the pattern in which it appears, the letters of the alphabet that form the word. The *signified* is the concept the pattern signifies.

For example, the letters spelling 'feet'[6] together form a signifier that indicates the concept of 'the lowest part of the leg on which the body stands and moves'. Thus, when the word is written or spoken it is a *sign* that means what it indicates. The *significance* is the relation between the signifier and the signified.

Although the signifier refers to the signified in order to be a full-fledged sign, the relationship of the signifier with the signified is merely *arbitrary* or conventional. This is a key insight into language and accounts for the diversity of signs that can mean the same signified by means of other signifiers (such as spoken and written words in other languages). Shakespeare said it long ago: 'What's in a name? That which we call a rose by any other name would smell as sweet.'[7]

Signs are not separate entities. They have *value* in their links to other signs. Meaning is the result of signs within a sign system or structure. Mere significance of a sign in isolation (the relation of the signifier to the signified within a sign) does not account for meaning unless it relates to other signs within a system. The word 'feet' would not be fully understood were it not related or contrasted with other signs such as 'toes', 'ankles', 'hands', 'head', and so on. Every sign needs a sign system to valorise its signification. Every sign is more than the sum of its parts. Saussure explains the relation between a sign and its system as follows:

> The notion of value…shows us that it is a great mistake to consider a sign as nothing more than the combination of a certain sound and a certain concept. To think of a sign as nothing more would be to isolate it from the system to which it belongs. It would be to suppose that a start could be made with individual signs, and a system constructed by putting them together. On the contrary, the system, a united whole, is the starting point from which it becomes possible, by a process of analysis, to identity its constituent elements.[8]

Barthes explains exactly how the spectrum of meaning unfolds from mere signification to whole systems that valorise signs through culture. All signs reveal meaning at three levels or orders of signification. The first, based on the Saussurean model of signification, Barthes calls 'denotation'. The second, he refers to as 'connotation' or 'myth'. He also suggests a third order of signification which he calls 'ideology' or 'mythology'.

Denotation/Sign

Barthes considers the isolated sign as a signifier denoting the signified. Continuing with the above example, the word 'feet' denotes the 'the lowest part of the leg on which the body stands and moves'. The denoted is the concept. The signifier that denotes is the form through which the denotation is visibly/phonetically expressed. Together, they form the one denoted *sign* (Figure 2.1). Barthes cautions that all three elements are important because 'we are dealing, in any semiological system, not with two, but with three different terms. For what we grasp is not at all one term after the other, but the correlation which unites them'.[9]

This 'first order signification' is called denotation. But there is a difference in denotation among signs. As Saussure declares, there are signs that are constituted by an arbitrary relationship between the signifier and the signified, that is, by an arbitrary correlation but not by cause and effect. Words in language are the result of arbitrary correlations accepted by convention. It matters little whether the sign for the 'lowest part of the leg' is 'feet' or 'piedi' or 'pai'. All one needs is conventional approval to sanction the existence of such signs, which are therefore called *conventional signs*.

Figure 2.1: Denotation/Sign

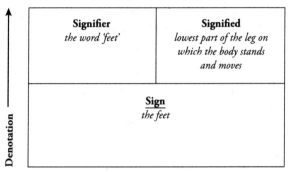

Source: Peter Gonsalves, adapted from R. Barthes, *The Fashion System* (Berkeley: University of California Press, 1990), 27–31.

Barthes's concern, however, was to apply Saussure's linguistic semiotics to everyday non-verbal things. He accepted Saussure's claim that in language, the relation between signifiers and signifieds is arbitrary. He admitted that non-verbal or *iconic signs* did seem to share a cause–effect relationship between signifier and signified. The signified (content) exerts a strong constraint on the signifier (form). Iconic signs were therefore 'quasi-arbitrary' or 'motivated', and not arbitrary or conventional.

For example, a photograph of my feet is a perfect iconic sign. The printed image of my feet is directly related to or motivated by my real feet. The photograph is not an arbitrary signifier like the word 'feet'. It is the effect of a mechanical recording of my flesh-and-bones feet. It does not require convention to validate that the photographic signifier is identified with the signified. In his *Mythologies*, Barthes gives us many examples of the iconic sign, one of which is Thauvin, a wrestler at a wrestling match. He describes the body of Thauvin as being so repugnant at the very first look, that it provoked nausea in the audience. The relation between the body of Thauvin as signifier and the concept of 'vileness' as signified was too obvious to be deemed arbitrary.[10]

Connotation/Myth/Symbol

A sign, at the level of denotation or the first order of signification, may seem neutral or inanimate, incapable of more than a literal, denotative meaning. Yet all signs, whether verbal or non-verbal, are part of a system within which the full potential of their denotations can be realised through a process called connotation. Here, the denotative sign (both signifier and signified together) is used as a signifier for an additional signified (Figure 2.2). Barthes calls this new signification 'myth'. Elsewhere in this work I have preferred to use the word 'symbol'.[11]

Figure 2.2: Connotation /Myth / Symbol

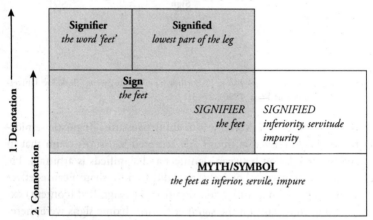

Source: Peter Gonsalves, adapted from R. Barthes, *The Fashion System* (Berkeley: University of California Press, 1990), 27–31.

> It can be seen that in myth there are two semiological systems, one of which is staggered in relation to the other: a linguistic system, the language (or the modes of representation which are assimilated to it), which I shall call the language-object, because it is the language which a myth gets hold of in order to build its own system; and myth itself, which I shall call metalanguage, because it is a second language, in which one speaks about the first.[12]

The level of connotation is the stage where the primary meaning of a sign is loaded with multiple mythic meanings that need not necessarily be consistent with the original first order of significance.

The second order allows the sign of the first order to go beyond its inherent significance and to find symbolical value in relation to other signs. Feet do not merely denote or point to the 'lowest part of the leg on which the body stands and moves'. Within a system of signs, the sign called 'feet' is 'staggered' into other signs, such as 'lowest part' signifying inferior position or 'the part that stands and moves' signifying 'the part that serves the rest of the body', or 'the part that touches the earth' signifying the part that is easily soiled and therefore dirty. The sign 'feet' now has new mythic meanings that accrue to its denotation: 'dirtiness, inferiority and servitude'.

From where do these mythic, second order significations emerge, if not from culture? Myths or symbols bring reality 'out there' in line with cultural and historical conditionings that are not mere linguistic meanings. Their meanings are intrinsically connected to values, emotions and attitudes. A photograph of my feet—which we had seen earlier as a pure denotative iconic sign—is now a sign that is *connoted*, that is laden with many meanings within a particular culture simply through its position, colour, level of adornment, gender, background, lighting effects, distance from the camera, angle, focus, objects surrounding it, and so on. Connotation, symbolisation or myth-making involves subjective involvement in the expression of meaning in contrast to denotation that is the result of mere detached naming. Denotation is about *what* things mean. Connotation is about *how* things mean.

> Myth is a system of communication, [...] it is a message. This allows one to perceive that myth cannot possibly be an object, a concept, or an idea; it is a mode of signification, a form [...]. Myth is not defined by the object of its message, but by the way in which it utters this message [...]. A tree is a tree. Yes, of course. But a tree as expressed by Minou Drouet is no longer quite a tree, it is a tree which is decorated, adapted to a certain type of consumption, laden with literary self-indulgence, revolt, images, in short, with a type of social usage which is added to pure matter.[13]

Ideology/Mythology

In his writings Barthes points to a 'third semiological chain'[14] or third order of signification constituted by the combination of the first two orders. In this third order of signification we shift our perspective from the sign as an independent entity to the realm of subjective responses (Figure 2.3).

But these responses are not individualistic in nature. They are shared responses between members of a culture. They are intersubjective responses which are culturally determined because through them cultural

Figure 2.3: Ideology/Mythology

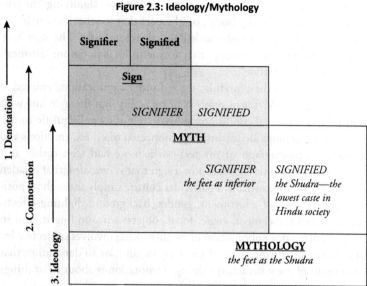

Source: Peter Gonsalves, adapted from R. Barthes, *The Fashion System* (Berkeley: University of California Press, 1990), 27–31.

membership is expressed. In the third order of signification, the sign reveals its membership to a *culturally ordered symbolic sign system*. The myths that operate within this cultural intersubjectivity are organised coherently to produce a meaning system called mythology or ideology.

Here signs reflect socially and politically dominant cultural concepts that underpin a particular world view. They serve the ideological function of *naturalisation*.[15] Their task surpasses that of connotation. They now naturalise the cultural by turning connotative myths, attitudes and behaviours, values and beliefs, cultural and historical interpretations into natural, normal, self-evident, eternal, commonsense ideologies. Myths function to hide the ideological meanings by turning them into that which 'goes without saying'.

Mythologies control social behaviour precisely because they are commonly and unquestionably accepted as true. Attempts to demystify or decode them would seem, at the least, foolish or useless and at the worst, anarchistic and subversive. The dominant institutions and mainstream channels of communication tend to promote a society's mythology because it is representative of the mind of the majority or dominant group that controls it.

The second order signification of inferiorised, servile and impure feet is not an isolated symbol or myth, but forms part of a larger mythology or ideology. It is a way of looking, not merely at the feet, but at those to whom the feet symbol is applied, backed by an ideology, in this case, promoted by Hindu scripture and tradition. The word 'feet', an innocent denotation of the lowest part of the legs on which any person stands and moves, is used to symbolise the Shudra, the lowest group in the Hindu Caste System (*Varnavyavastha*). The cultural influences of the third order of signification lifts the innocent biological sign/denotation to a level infused with prejudicial myths/connotations to a mythology/ideology in which discriminatory perceptions, attitudes and behaviours of Hindu society towards persons of the Shudra caste are naturalised.

It must be stated, in conclusion, that the semiotic analysis of the three orders of significance presented here is an exercise in the structural dissection of signs, myths and mythologies. In reality the lines of distinction are often blurred. Conventional and iconic signs, myths and connotations, first, second and third orders of signification merge into each other in daily perception and discourse.

Oriental Dress and the Three Orders of Signification

It is time to apply Barthes's three orders of signification to a concrete instance from early 20th century colonial culture. Much of what was written, drawn and photographed in this period was the work of colonialists. Their reconstructions of the Indian reality were never purely denotative. If one were to focus on their sartorial representations alone, one would be alarmed by the extent of myth-making involved. It was not as if the British discovered an India 'out there', detached and disconnected from their perceptions of it. Their perceptions of India were to a large extent the India they chose to see and to mythologise for their benefit.

The India they chose to see is best described by Jawaharlal Nehru:

I remember that when I was a boy the British-owned newspapers in India were full of official news and utterances; of service news, transfers and promotions; of the doings of English society, of polo, races, dances, and amateur theatricals. There was hardly a word about the people of India, about their political, cultural, social, or economic life. Reading them one would hardly suspect that they existed.[16]

The India they mythologised was an exotic oriental exhibit meant to project England as the world's foremost Universal Empire on which 'the sun never sets'.[17] This, despite the fact that the majority of the 300 million inhabitants were burdened with the ravages of famine, unemployment and neglect.

Thanks to the Indian rebellion of 1857, the East India Company was terminated and its territories and powers were brought directly under the British Empire's control. The military was among the first to experience the changes in imperial policy. The British decided to rule in an 'oriental manner' with strength and with expectation of instant obedience, but also with a fantasised notion of what an 'oriental' warrior should look like.[18] Thus, colourful turbans were introduced. Dress included knee-length tunics in bright hues, breeches and high boots. Parades and ceremonial functions celebrated the grand display of oriental military clothing.

The first major demonstration of the new imperial paradigm was in 1876, during the visit of the Prince of Wales to India. The princes of India presented themselves before the Prince in regal splendour—a variety of clothes, a riot of colours and an extraordinary array of precious stones and jewellery.[19] The pomp and pageantry so fascinated Queen Victoria that she suggested an official dress uniform for her Indian civil servants as well—a suggestion that was never translated into law due to the exorbitant expense it would entail.[20]

It did not seem to matter that 1876 was the year the Great Indian Famine began, costing more than 5 million lives.[21]

Another example of mythologising Indian dress to feed British perceptions and definitions of normal Indian society is Gandhi's own experience at Lord Curzon's *Darbar*:

> Some Rajas and Maharajas who had been invited to the darbar were members of the Club. In the Club I always found them wearing fine Bengalee *dhoti*s and shirts and scarves. On the darbar day they put on trousers befitting *khansama*s [waiters] and shining boots. I was pained and inquired of one of them the reason for the change.

> 'We alone know our unfortunate condition. We alone know the insults we have to put up with, in order that we may possess our wealth and titles,' he replied.

'But what about these *khansama* turbans and these shining boots?' I asked.

'Do you see any difference between *khansama*s and us?' he replied, and added, 'they are our *khansama*s, we are Lord Cruzon's *khansama*s. If I were to absent myself from the levee, I should have to suffer the consequences. If I were to attend it in my usual dress, it would be an offence. And do you think I am going to get any opportunity there of talking to Lord Curzon? Not a bit of it!'

I was moved to pity for this plainspoken friend.[22]

Gandhi was sad to see how the English authorities had abused the refinery of Indian dress to decorate their lavish dinners with no respect for the feelings of the princes who wore them. On another occasion he saw the Maharajas 'bedecked like women, (in) silk pyjamas and silk *achakans*[23], pearl necklaces round their necks, bracelets on their wrists, pear and diamond tassels on their turbans and, besides all this, swords with golden hilts hanging from their waist bands'.[24] On further inquiry, Gandhi realised that the fancy clothing was their obligatory dress code for such occasions, even though some Maharajas had a positive dislike for these 'badges of impotence'.[25]

The original denotations of princely power were used as a platform on which to graft a completely different connotation. From the once exalted personalities that commanded obeisance, the Indian princes were reduced to effeminate items of ornamentation in a mythology that was construed and controlled by their colonial lords.

Barthes' Semiology of Clothing

In the foreword to *The Fashion System*, Barthes identifies the characteristic quality of his work: 'This study actually addresses neither clothing nor language but the "translation," so to speak, of one into the other, insofar as the former is already a system of signs.'[26] The word 'system' defines Barthes's field of study. It was a field that affected French intellectual life after World War II and that came to be known as 'structuralism'. Both these words, 'system' and 'structure' indicate the logical priority of the whole over its parts. The structuralists insist that whole and parts can be properly explained only in terms of the relations that exist between parts. The essential quality of the structuralist method and its fundamental tenet lies in its attempt to study not just the elements of a whole, but the complex network of relationships that link and unite those elements.[27]

Collective organisation is therefore essential to the fulfilment of individual and social needs. Clothing is one such need, just like politics, economics, culture and aesthetics. Because of the interdependency of these parts, each area of human life has to be studied from an interdisciplinary perspective. Only in this way will knowledge contribute to a better understanding of the whole of human existence.

Consequent on this structuralist perspective of human existence, Barthes leans on Marxian economics to understand the semiotics of clothing.[28] Economic activity, he says, can be understood as constituting three dimensions: production, distribution and consumption (Table 2.1). Production deals with the manufacture of an object; distribution, with the processes involved in making it reach people willing to have it; and consumption refers to ways in which the object is used by those who buy it.[29] Seen from a sartorial viewpoint, he calls these three dimensions in the journey through the fashion system, 'the real garment', 'the represented garment' and 'the used garment'. These are not three distinct garments but three modalities that any garment assumes while passing through the stages of production, distribution and consumption. Barthes' methodology for analysing these three stages is the three orders of signification explained earlier in this chapter. The following table puts the general plan of his sartorial signification in perspective.

In its first modality, clothing is the real garment—the sensorial object that is a sign of its bare existence at the first phase in an economic system called production. It concerns the manufacture of cloth, the properties that give cloth its distinct quality, and the way cloth is stitched together to produce ready-to-wear clothing. Here clothing as a sign is merely that

Table 2.1: Three Modalities of Clothing in the Fashion System

1. Production	The REAL garment	Denotation—Sign
2. Distribution	The REPRESENTED garment	Connotation—Myth
3. Consumption	The USED garment	Ideology—Mythology

Source: Author.

which covers, protects and adorns the body. This is the raw untouched-by-myth stage in the first order of significance.

The second modality of clothing is that which is grafted on to the first. It is where connotation takes over, where the represented garment comes into existence, where myth-making, creativity and articulation take off into flights of fantasy, imagery and verbosity. Here the real clothing is transformed into a fashion object due to the economic exigencies of marketing and distributing. The continuous flow of myths is an entertaining façade to speed up consumption. Clothes take time to wear out. Without the myths of fashion, people would be content with what they have, and would probably take a year or two before they bought new clothes.

The third modality is the used garment, that which is bought and consumed for daily use. It is the phase that naturalises one's way of being, thinking and doing. It is the third order of signification that develops ideologies to maintain and defend the status quo. The once fashion object is now customised and absorbed by culture. It is not perceived as fashionable anymore but as '*the* way to do things', as 'that which goes without saying', as mythology that is co-opted by all. Just as greater production needs greater distribution and vice versa, greater distribution depends on greater consumption and vice versa. The wheels of the system continue to churn while myth after newer myth applies the grease to make it all seem innocent and naturally repeatable.

'[T]he circulation of Fashion thus relies in large part on an activity of *transformation*'[30] from the technological garment to its iconic and verbal representation, from its connotation to its mythology. Once the real garment appears as a representation it is a changed entity—it is no more the manufactured garment but the 'fashion object' itself. When the fashion object is accepted by the majority, it is no more 'in fashion' but has become normalised routine.

Clothing: Real and Represented

Having briefly mapped out various elements in the phenomenon we call fashion we need to understand how these elements enter into relationships of mutual dependency so as 'to reconstitute step by step a system of meaning' as it is laid out in *articulated language*.[31] The object of Barthes's study is therefore fashion magazines, that is, clothing as represented, not real clothing. What are his reasons for this choice?

The link between the real and the represented garment is important, otherwise it would be difficult to understand the clothing system. It is customary to separate the real from the represented, placing, as it were, the actual object (clothing) on one side, and the language used to describe it (written-clothing or image-clothing) on the other. However, this distinction denies an epistemological truth: the intimate, almost intrinsic link between a system of objects and the language used to articulate it.[32] Our common experience shows that it is impossible to signify an object without talking about it. Semiology is a necessary part of linguistics. By studying the written and imaged expressions of fashion to unravel the Fashion system, Barthes is demonstrating the indispensable link between a system as the object of analysis and a system as the subject of communication:

> If we go beyond a few rudimentary signs […] can clothing signify without recourse to the speech that describes it, comments upon it, and provides it with signifiers and signifieds abundant enough to constitute a system of meaning? Man is doomed to articulated language, and no semiological undertaking can ignore this fact […]. [T]his work's essential function is to suggest that in a society like ours, where myths and rite have assumed the form of a reason, i.e., ultimately of a discourse, human language is not only the model of meaning but its very foundation.[33]

In showing the important link between a system and its discourse, Barthes justifies his methodology that purports to move backwards, from an elaboration of the discourse of clothing (represented in writings or images) to the actual or real clothing itself.

Barthes notes that in fashion magazines, the clothing that is represented is always in the form of an image accompanied by a text. Represented clothing is therefore of two types: there is image-clothing accompanied by written-clothing.[34] Each of these exists in relation to what Barthes calls the 'real garment' (Figure 2.4).[35]

Image-clothing and written-clothing have different structures. In image-clothing the substances are forms, lines, surfaces, colours and the relation is spatial. In written-clothing the substance is words and the relation between them is logical or syntactical. The first structure is

Figure 2.4: Real and Represented Clothing

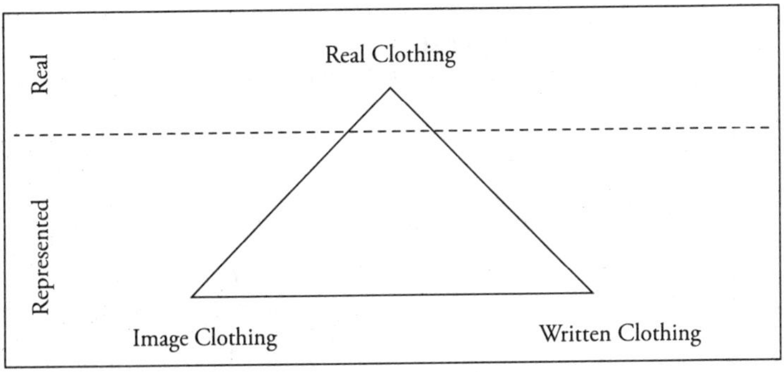

Source: Author.

'plastic', the second verbal.[36] Instead, the structure of the real garment, which is 'the model which guides the information transmitted by the first two garments', is technological.[37]

Each of these three structures of clothing must be known through different means. In the case of real clothing, it must be known not merely by sight, for its visual image does not reveal all its intricacies. It must be known through the mechanical process of its production, that is, at the level of its manufacture. This technological level is fundamental; Barthes refers to it as the 'mother tongue', of which the other two levels are only derived languages or 'translations'.[38] But why are translations needed at all? Is not a literal denotative articulation of real clothing sufficient? What other significance is necessary over and above that which real clothing already signifies? Barthes's second order of significance reveals the answer:

> Real clothing is burdened with practical considerations (protection, modesty, adornment); these finalities disappear from 'represented' clothing, which no longer serve to protect, to cover, or to adorn, but at most to *signify* protection, modesty, or adornment; [...] if the magazine describes a certain article of clothing verbally, it does so solely to convey a message whose content is: Fashion.[39]

In other words, the denotative concept of 'clothing' becomes the culturally connoted concept of fashion in the second order of signification (Figure 2.5).

Figure 2.5: Clothing, Denotation and Connotation

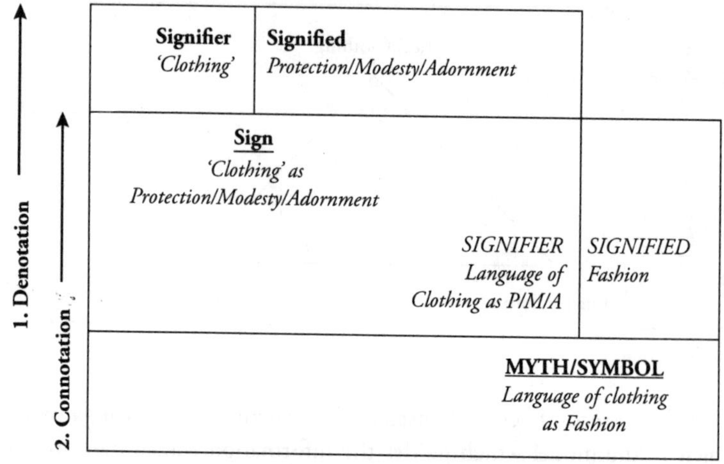

Signifier 'Clothing'	Signified Protection/Modesty/Adornment	
Sign 'Clothing' as Protection/Modesty/Adornment	SIGNIFIER Language of Clothing as P/M/A	SIGNIFIED Fashion
	MYTH/SYMBOL Language of clothing as Fashion	

(Left axis: 1. Denotation, 2. Connotation)

Source: Peter Gonsalves adapted from R. Barthes, *The Fashion System* (Berkeley: University of California Press, 1990), 27–31.

It is not a question of its temporal origins but of the meaning of fashion in the modern world. Barthes breaks from tradition that holds on to real clothing as anterior to its representation. As far as fashion is concerned the words and images (especially words) are active agents that communicate the real garment much more than the real garment itself. Articulated language or speech is the 'inevitable relay for any signifying order'.[40] Clothing cannot signify without having recourse to description and commentary through words. Thus, the consumer never encounters the real garment, but the fashionable object—the garment as myth. The consumer first meets the garment in its already 'translated' form, as already 'invested with meaning'. Thus, in analysing real clothing, as Barthes does, it makes sense to proceed from discourse about clothing (the represented, mythic garment) to the reality constituted by such discourse.[41]

Clothing: Represented and Used

The used garment is the life of clothing after it has been purchased. It is the garment of everyday routine and not-so-routine socialisation. It is the 'stuff' of sartorial choices and how they are conditioned and shaped as a result of ideological and socio-cultural influences. The used garment is therefore the clothing at the third level of signification—when a type of cloth or clothing is accepted as part of the system in conformity with an ideology. Although Barthes' *The Fashion System* says little about the used garment, other writings on fashion[42] as well as his general approach to the connotative dimensions of meaning will help complement what is lacking.

Saussure had distinguished between language and speech:

> Language is an institution, an abstract body of constraints; speech is the momentary part of this institution which the individual extracts and actualizes for purposes of communication; language issues from the mass of spoken words and yet all speech is itself drawn from language, in history this is a dialectic between the structure and the event, and in communication theory between the code and the message.[43]

Barthes applies this distinction to clothing. Written-clothing is like language because descriptions of clothing are likewise based on the constraints that make the garment in question fashionable. The written-clothing is the structural, institutional form of what is worn. It provides the grammar of fashion. However, when this institutional form (like speech) is actualised, when an individual wears this institutional grammar on his/her person we have *dress*. When Barthes is referring to used clothing he is referring to both, the institutionalised fashion as well as to the individualised dress, the latter being the actualised instance of the former (as the spoken word is to language). In society there usually exists a lively interaction between these two poles.

Thus, the used garment is a cyclic process between clothing and dress: individually actualised dress codes are institutionally accepted to the point of becoming standard clothing, costume or uniform; institutionally accepted clothing imposes a respect for psycho-social conformity on the individual's choice of dress. This mutual exchange between clothing and dress highlights the importance of clothing as a social and semiotic system or, in a word, a 'sociologic'[44] system. The used garment is essentially a 'fashion object', a phenomenon that has collective, organised, formal and normative sanction.[45]

Finally, what value does Barthes give to the myth on which the fashion system thrives? Clothing that is rich in verbal connotation, the one from which Barthes draws out an elaborate structural analysis of written fashion, is an important part of the journey from its manufacture and denotative conceptions of real clothing to the socially naturalised systems of use. Myth is 'an important part' because, even if the garment remained only descriptive and imaginary, that is, without any relation to real or used clothing, it would still shape and determine mass culture. The fashion object is the most determining factor in the life of clothing: it saves raw or real clothing from anonymity and used or normalised clothing from routine.

Barthes's study is a plea for a deeper analysis of the mass systems of collective representation (the reconstructions of mass media) and for recognising these systems as social facts with their own specific structures and operations.[46] Contrarily, the linguistic structure of the fashion analysed by Barthes in *The Fashion System*, although complete in scope and content, cannot be fully comprehended if divorced from the larger sartorial social structure that forms the basis and background of his thesis. Figure 2.6 illustrates Barthes's insight into clothing and fashion as two independent yet complementary systems of mass culture.

Figure 2.6: The Fashion Object

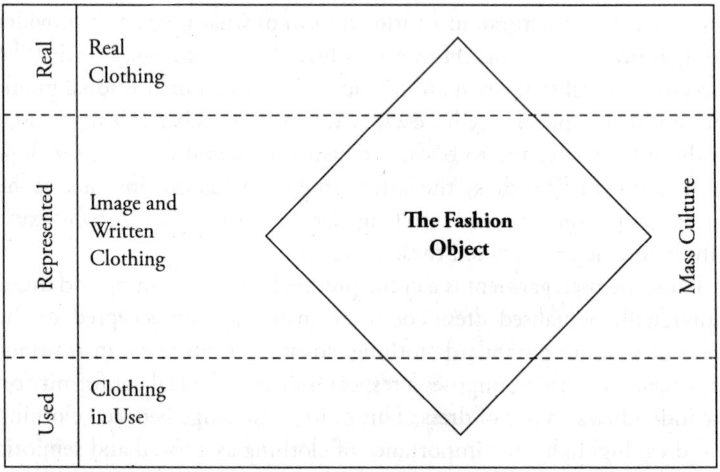

Source: Author.

The Real, Represented and Used Garment in Colonial India

Barthes's semiotics of clothing provides us with some fresh insights into the sartorial history of colonial India. In the pre-Gandhian era the real garment was a combination of Indian and English labour with the economic benefits tipped disproportionately in favour of the latter. Overseen by the British Raj, the raw cotton would be baled off to English mills by Indian merchants in a climate of stiff competition for maximum production and cheaper labour—to the detriment of the Indian cotton-growing farmers and cotton-picking labourers who toiled ceaselessly in hot tropical conditions. Hand spinning and weaving of cotton cloth on the subcontinent had all but disappeared. To add insult to injury, the mill-manufactured textile was sold back to India for mass consumption.[47]

However, the oppressive capacity of clothing did not lie only in real clothing, that is, the way it was manufactured. The manner it was represented in texts and images and the sanction these representations received in public regulation and custom constituted a more invidious and pervasive form of control. Some basic questions underpinning the 'sanctioned' represented garment or the 'fashion object' are: who controlled the representations, in whose interests and for what purpose.

The strategies through which real clothing was converted into the 'fashion object' of mass culture via networks of distribution and consumption were as important a means of subjugating the colonised as the technological process of the real garment itself. It is therefore important to look at some examples of represented clothing in the pre-Gandhian era. They will reveal the subtle role played by imperialism's mass cultural ideology in determining what was the officially promoted fashion object for both colonisers and the colonised, and how it was naturalised through the used garment that was unquestioningly accepted by the gentry.

A market research on the Indian customer and designing the myth

One method of controlling India was to improve the British producer's knowledge of Indian sartorial tastes in view of making India a mass consumer of British textiles. John Forbes Watson's extensive single-volume study, *The Textile Manufactures and Costumes of the People of India*, was written in 1866 with precisely such an objective. He had earlier produced 18 volumes of 700 samples of Indian textiles that were to be regarded as 'textile museums'. He thought it necessary that the mills of

Lancashire shape their production to target the poorer rural classes of India and not the educated urbanites because the manufacture of lower quality cloth for mass consumption was more profitable than that of higher quality cloth for just a few elite. He therefore deemed it essential that clothing tastes and designs of the Indian masses be thoroughly known: 'how the garment was worn, by which sex and for what purpose,' as well as 'the relationship between the size of the cloth, its decoration and use'.[48] According to him, 'India is in a position to become a magnificent customer [...]. *What is wanted and what to be copied to meet that want* is thus accessible for study in these museums.'[49] Watson also stated that increased consumption of European cloth in India would be good for both the Manchester manufactures and the people of India, who, he felt, were under-clothed and to whom cheap textiles would be a great boon. Thus, in serving British interests, Indian interests were also served. If, however, the Indian weavers could not compete with the cheapness of British cloth it would not be a bad thing if their labour in so vast and resourceful a country be diverted 'into other and perhaps more profitable channels [...] sufficient to occupy the energies of her whole people'.[50]

Watson's work flourished and his rationale dominated British business perspectives, the results of which were evident. His sharply focused production and distribution plan boosted the consumption of British cotton cloth exports to India. The increase between 1849 to 1889 was from just over £2 million to just under £27 million a year.[51]

Civilising the Indian customer and the boundaries of myth-making

It may seem paradoxical that while the British wanted the majority of Indians to buy English cloth they discouraged the full appropriation of exclusive English attire by elite Indians. They strove to hold on jealously to their cultural standards of fashion and feared that by sharing it with brown-bodied Indians their cherished values would be compromised. Historical studies on the verbal and pictorial literature of the late 19th and early 20th centuries reveal this duplicity of British motives regarding Indians as mass consumers of British culture but not as cultural equals.

A favourite theme was the Bengali 'baboo'. A caricature entitled, 'The Baboo's progress or what we are coming to!'[52] shows Bengalis usurping roles hitherto reserved for the British alone. For instance, the English are seen at the beck and call of the brown *baboo*s who are elegantly attired in English dress. They dance to the tune of the Bengalis, are arrested and tried by them, serve them as drivers, personal attendants, shoe-shiners, soldiers and humble subjects. The artist satirises the British fear of what would ultimately happen if Indians were allowed to share the same cultural privileges of the British race. It is an illustration intended to shock the English reader into preventing Indians from imitating British ways.

From a Barthesian perspective, such illustrations would not have shocked the British reader if the politically correct ideology of English society were represented: where the English are firmly in control of their socio-cultural superiority and where Indians are shown as subservient and at the beck and call of their imperial masters. Such a 'correct' representation would be the naturalised 'mythology', the ideology which 'goes without saying', the type of behaviour and dress that received collective and formal sanction by the Empire.

Nirad Chaudhuri, a Bengali baboo, sums up the subaltern viewpoint under the British Raj as follows: 'They, the British, were violently repelled by English in our mouths and even more violently by English clothes on our backs.'[53]

Footwear and the problem of multicultural decoding

Often lack of clarity in reading cultural signs led to social and legal difficulties. Even in such cases, British legislation, often favouring British interests, determined what practices were mandatory and what were not. One example worth noting is the use of footwear. In European cultures a person is shown respect by the tipping of the hat, while footwear is retained at all times—a custom suitable for the intemperate weather of Europe. Indian culture, on the contrary, coherent with a tropical climate, allows for the use of open footwear and consequently considers the baring of one's feet as a mark of deference—not the removal of caps or turbans. This practice of removing footwear on entering another's house, or at a *darbar*, or on entering a temple, irked the British:

> The British rules governing the wearing or non-wearing of shoes was that Europeans did not have to conform to Indian custom, but Indians had to conform to European ideas of what was proper Indian behavior. The

Europeans could also decide when an Indian practice had changed sufficiently to allow their subjects to follow new rules.[54]

Brown bodies in white men's clothes and the myths of civility

If the British manipulated the use of Indian clothing to serve their interests, so did elite Indians in the use of English attire. By the late 19th century, British dress was looked upon as the normative representation of civility. Indians perceived in English dress a certain dignity that they found lacking in their own cultural costumes. When an Indian donned European clothing he not only felt respected, but he also felt himself a class above his fellow countrymen. In his own eyes he considered himself to be on par with Europeans, worthy of social intercourse with Englishmen and women. His new appropriated identity was an escape from the 'stigma' of his real Indianness.

However, the exercise was a failure. Many who dressed as Europeans had to face the ridicule of the British who were disdainful of an Indian body in British garb. For the British, their attire was not merely a manifestation of superior quality fashion, it was more importantly a symbol of their self-perception as a superior *race*. Clothing was their second skin, non-transferable without their consent. The 'fashionable object', the signifier, and the racial substrata, the signified, were one undivided symbol of superiority. This is why Indians in British garments were made to feel that *they*, because of their Indian racial identity, were too inferior to signify the superiority that European clothes signified. They were not worthy to own or borrow the 'collective, organised, formal and normative sanction' that British clothes represented on British bodies. And since the colonisers decided what was 'good' for the colonised, their sanction or lack of it was the norm.

English clothing and the mythology of contamination

One factor that kept the English rigid in their use of English dress was the mythology of contamination. Copiously written treatises published from London emphasised caution in matters of clothes, food, health and hygiene.[55] The title of the book published in 1813 by James

Johnson sums up the general fear: *The Influence of Tropical Climates, especially the Climate of India on European Constitutions; and the Principal Effects and Diseases thereby Induced, their Prevention or Removal and the Means of Preserving Health in Hot Countries, Rendered Obvious to Europeans of Every Capacity.*

The book suggested various means of protection from perspiration, sun-stroke, dust, dirt and contamination. One advice it offered was to clothe oneself well from head to foot. Huge quantities of clothes were suggested for both men and women who planned to live in India. Here is a sample list of men's wear for the voyage by Captain Thomas Williamson: 48 shirts, an equal number of undershirts, four pairs of pantaloons plus an unspecified number when he reaches India, woven cotton underwear, 72 pairs of stockings, 24 white Irish linen waistcoats, two or three jackets, several pairs of boots and shoes.[56] John Borthwick Gilchrist produced a list entitled 'Necessaries for a Lady Proceeding to India,' with these details: 72 chemises, 36 night gowns, 36 night caps, three flannel petticoats, 12 middle flannel petticoats without bodies, 12 slips, 62 pairs of stockings, 30 dresses, 60 pocket handkerchiefs, four dressing gowns, three bonnets, 12 morning caps, 24 pairs of long gloves, 24 pairs of short gloves, four corsets.[57]

Underlying this preoccupation for clothing were various theories of perspiration that determined even the type of cloth materials used. Johnson discouraged the use of linen, as it retained perspiration and was likely to occasion a chill. Gilchrist favoured flannel and so did many manuals because flannel used at all times is 'an excellent protection against sudden alternations of weather.'[58]

How is it that Europeans did not ask why Indians could live with simple clothes and without flannels to protect themselves from the harsh Indian climate? Theories were developed that gradually became standard mythologies that justified the white man's comfort at the brown man's expense. Dr Johnson declared that Indian anatomy, skin and physiology were different from the European. Nature had provided the Indian with a skin 'colour and texture' and 'extreme vessels' (pores) that 'are neither so violently stimulated by the heat, nor so easily struck torpid by sudden transitions to cold'. The theory explained that Indians perspired differently from Europeans because Indians 'secrete a very different kind of fluid being more of an oily and tenacious nature than the sweat of the European'.[59] Thanks to this difference, Europeans could depend on

Indian labour and, as the colonial masters, had a right to demand such dependence. Furthermore, the theory stated that the white man's prime requisite for good health was the avoidance of strenuous activity in the heat of the sun. It was for this reason that 'an army of dark-skinned servants was required to relieve the sahib of strenuous work'.[60] The Englishman's entourage of personal Indian servants or 'coolies' is a stereotypical representation reflected famously in novels, paintings, photographs and films.

Swadeshi—a Gandhian 'Fashion System'

Gandhi's Swadeshi Movement was founded on the real garment. He initiated a programme where cotton cultivation was followed by picking, ginning, carding, combing, spinning and weaving—processes undertaken chiefly through the manual labour of poor peasants and their families in distant villages and towns of India. The *charkha* was reintroduced and promoted through training programmes. It was to be the alternative to industrialised mass production affected through English and Indian mills.

These two prototypes of the 'real-garment', that is, mill-made cloth and home-spun *khadi*, were two radically divergent socio-economic approaches to the one Indian reality: the former had reduced India to a feeder of its own imperial subjugation; the latter would steadily propel India towards freedom, sustainability and self-respect. Gandhi's ingenious insight was to discover the potential of clothing's subversive power exactly from the site where the Empire had earlier grasped the potential of clothing's power to subjugate—the *technological processes* of cloth manufacture, or in Barthes's terminology, real cloth.

But Gandhi's personal struggle with clothing choices, his extensive reading of the consequences of colonialism on the Indian economy, and his observation of English custom and manners led him further. He strove to provide an alternative to the sartorial dilemmas that kept the English in 'their insularity and unimaginativeness'[61] and made educated Indians mindless imitators of English ways.

Through years of monopoly of the manufacture and distribution of cloth, the British had 'naturalised' the garment of industrialisation. Lancashire and Manchester were unquestionably the textile industries of the world. The first order of significance where the fabric first received its denotative value had already been clothed in myths of cultural and technological superiority. Connotations of civility and respectability attached to English cloth and clothing bypassed important questions about the history and eco-political consequences of cloth production such as: What shifts in cloth production had occurred? Why? Who controlled the production? What were the means and processes used? For what purposes was the production? Who benefited? At whose cost?

Gandhi thought it important to bring these questions of real clothing to the fore because they determined how one perceived stereotypical representations of civility and respectability. In seeking answers to real clothing questions, he believed, he would find the solution to new and appropriate[62] representations of clothing for his people. He was also convinced that if his solution was accepted, it would ignite a new economic vision in which an alternative significance of clothing would pave the way for a countrywide mass movement for social change, one that would have the potential of aborting the imperial stranglehold over India at its very base, that is, at the level of eco-political sartorial control. The new signification thus created would fashion an independent, productive and self-reliant India. He called this new 'semiologics',[63] this node where the sociology of real cloth would meet the semiotics of representative clothing, *swadeshi*. It would be an alternative clothing system, a Gandhian 'fashion system' one might say, that would promote through cloth and clothing an economic self-sufficiency (*swadeshi*) powerful enough to establish self-government (*swaraj*).

The ideological foundation for such an alternative clothing system had already been established by the early Indian nationalists during the first Swadeshi Movement of 1903. It was based on the nexus between the economics and semiotics of cloth and drew its dominant ideology from Dadabhai Naoroji's 'Drain Theory'. However, the supply of cloth made from Indian mills and handloom weavers was not enough to clothe the participating masses. Moreover, some nationalists continued to wear British textiles and English costumes. This gave rise to fundamental inconsistencies in real and represented clothing:

> A fascinating paradox was generated from the semiotic and economic characteristics of cloth. These early nationalists wanted to revive and modernize Indian manufactures, especially the textile industry. But their political beliefs stood in the way of utilizing its products. Cloth is made

to be worn and to express the social identity of the wearer. They expressed their belief in English values and their right to English justice by comporting themselves as English gentlemen in English dress (albeit with special hat or turban to signify a slight cultural distinctiveness). Because they were still committed to this Englishness of dress they were incapable of carrying out their own program of *swadeshi*.[64]

In Barthes's terminology, the early nationalists chose a syntagmatic structure of *swadeshi*—one that wore Indian pieces of clothing alongside British dress with British conceptions of civility. Gandhi had passed through these phases while in South Africa.[65] When he returned to India in 1915 he discarded the juxtaposition of east and west clothing styles. He opted for a radically different solution, a paradigmatic change that would discard all foreign interpretations of dressing for respectability. The new east paradigm of clothing would take into consideration eco-political, psycho-cultural and socio-religious conceptions of Indianness. It would be a holistic interdisciplinary representation of clothing, something hitherto unexplored by previous national leaders. Nehru gives free rein to poetic nostalgia as he describes the paradigmatic originality of Gandhi's style:

> And then Gandhi came. He was like a powerful current of fresh air that made us stretch ourselves and take deep breaths; like a beam of light that pierced the darkness and removed the scales from our eyes; like a whirlwind that upset many things, but most of all the working of people's minds. He did not descend from the top; he seemed to emerge from the millions of India, speaking their language and incessantly drawing attention to them and their appalling condition. Get off the backs of these peasants and workers, he told us, all you who live by their exploitation; get rid of the system that produces their poverty and misery.[66]

Gandhi's radical shift to an alternative economics and signification of clothing set off a chain of cataclysmic reversals that redefined the meaning of power, progress and civility:

- *Who:* The ordinary Indian and not the English or the Indian-elite would control cloth production.
- *Where:* Simple homes in Indian villages, towns and cities would be the new centres of production, not the mills of Manchester, Lancashire, Bombay or Ahmedabad.

- *How:* The traditional *charkha* and not the modern mill would be the means used; the collaboration of the masses in production rather than mass production by a few would be the process involved.
- *What:* Homespun-*khadi* would be produced. It would be the symbolic fabric through which unity of purpose in non-cooperation and sustainability (*swadeshi*) would be expressed.
- *Why: Purna swaraj* and not imperial profits would be the ultimate aim of cloth production.
- *When:* The National Flag in *khadi* cloth would be emblematic of the people's hope in a proximate 'Independence day' when India would be free from Imperial control.
- *Process:* The creation of a new mentality to guide a new process that would be diametrically opposed to the hegemonic imperial or elitist model, where the *swadeshi* or *khadi* mentality, the 'decentralization of the production and distribution of the necessities of life' would be the foundation of the process, and where social change would begin in the remotest villages.[67]

Despite opposition from some Indian leaders, most took to *khadi* in support of the movement Gandhi had initiated. By 1921 all Congressmen were dressed in *khadi*. The governor of Bombay Presidency, Chittaranjan Das, made *khadi* the uniform of civic employees, fulfilling in an unexpectedly prophetic manner the desire Queen Victoria had expressed 45 years before: to orientalise the dress of Indian civil servants. The boycott and burning of foreign cloth and the growing network of hand spun *khadi* across India gave a visible face to the Civil Disobedience Movement and altered representations of civility: the civilised person was no longer one who dressed in English clothes, but the one who refused to cooperate with a Government that ruled through unjust laws; the civilised person was no longer the one who wore poor clothes, but the one willing to wear clothes made by the sweat of his brow. Gandhi's new clothing system had the power to signify a new civilisation freed from colonial oppression. Inso doing, he put an end to the imperial fashion system and its definition of civility by introducing his alternative system of *swadeshi*.

The liberative aspects of the *swadeshi* manner of dress will be appreciated better if observed against the backdrop of the larger fashion system he created from production, through distribution, to consumption (Table 2.2).

Table 2.2: The Fashion System under Imperialism and Gandhi

Under Imperialism	Under Gandhi
Production	
Centralised	Decentralised
Industrial manufacture	*Charkha* and hand-spinning
Capital intensive	Labour intensive
Mass-production in concentrated space	Production by dispersed masses
Wealth oriented	Quality of life oriented
Exploitation of many by few	Honest labour of all
Urban centred	Village based
Foreign or mill-made cloth	Home-spun *Khadi*
Social stability	Social instability
Changes accepted on British terms	Changes on Indian terms
Violence	Non-violence
Distribution	
Foreign cloth and clothes as Fashion	Foreign cloth and clothes as evil to be burnt
Comfortable lifestyle	Marches, picketing, demonstrations and arrests
Major cloth distributors and manufactures	Associations, volunteer organisations
Two types of cloth for rich and poor	Single cloth for all
Relatively cheap	Relatively expensive
Dressing for adornment	Dressing for solidarity and service
Promoting English fashion	Promoting *swadeshi* and *swaraj*
Ultimate goal: Profits and Indian domination	Ultimate goal: *purna swaraj*
Consumption	
English dress	Indian dress
British dress standards	Indian simplicity and neatness
Hats, sola *topis*	Turbans, Gandhi *topis*
Trousers, pantaloons	Pyjamas, *dhotis*
Frocks and skirts	*Saris*
Shoes, boots	Barefoot, sandals
Shirts, coats, jackets	*Kurtas, angarkas*, barebodied

(Contd.)

(Contd.)

Civility based on appearance	Civility based on morality and fair play
Greed	Need
Profit driven agenda	Equality and freedom driven agenda
Dignity, affluence, pride, inflexibility	Rectitude, simplicity, humility, adaptability
British cultural identity	Indian cultural identity

Source: Author.

The elements of this alternative system are arranged as binary opposites and may be read horizontally as paradigms that are mutually exclusive to each other. Hats cannot subsist with turbans, nor can trousers with *dhoti*s. A person may choose either one or the other, but never both at the same time.

They may also be read vertically as syntagmatic features proper to each of the two systems. Hats, trousers, shoes, can be produced from mill-made cloth with profit-driven agendas to promote the whole integrated system.

A glance at the two paradigms reveal strong differences. The elements of the two systems under imperialism and Gandhi are incompatible together. One must cede to the other.

In reading the table, three points of caution must be kept in mind. First, the two lists summarise ideal or official elaborations of the clothing systems; they do not refer to how the systems were actually realised in practice. Second, the exercise of contrasting the two clothing systems serves a didactic function and is not without the risk of simplification. Third, the lists are not exhaustive.

The interconnectedness within each fashion system manifests the coherence of the syntagmatic ensemble with the dominant ideology: the British imperial system set the target for worldwide definitions of civility and culture attracting educated urbanites to affluence and European ways; Gandhi's village-centred development demanded a dressing for simplicity, unity and truth in a land where millions needed food, labour, dignity and freedom. The practical implications of sartorial choices in a context of heightened political pressure and unprecedented mass-awakening meant either favouring the Empire or subverting it, seeking its patronage or risking imprisonment, saving one's life or losing it.

It was difficult to sustain the normalcy of the imperial fashion system once Gandhi came. He challenged his people to adopt his alternative myth and its values of unity, dignity and freedom. Caught between the two conflicting fashion systems, all Indians were forced to reveal whether they were for imperialism or for independence simply by dressing the way they chose. *The sartorial became the political.*

Notes

1. Roland Barthes, *Image, Music, Text*, tr. Stephen Heath, (London: Fontana Press, 1977), 146.
2. In 1969 the IASS–AIS (International Association of Semioticians Studies–Association Internationale de Sémiotique) decided against differentiating between the two terms, semiology (the linguistic tradition of Ferdinand de Saussure) and semiotica (the philosophical tradition of Charles Peirce), in favour of preserving a unitary meaning among the many authors who investigate the nature of signs, their impact on society and the laws that govern them. Cf. Umberto Eco, *Trattato di Semiotica Generale* (Milano: Bompiani, 1994), 13.
3. Barthes, 'Le Grain de la voix,' 8 /15, cited in Jonathan Culler, *Barthes*, ed. Jonathan Culler (Oxford: Oxford University Press, 2002), 7.
4. Roland Barthes, *Système de la Mode* (Paris: Editions du Seuil, 1967). (Although first published in 1967, his ideas developed a decade earlier.) In this study, we refer to the English translation by M. Ward and R. Howard, *The Fashion System* (Berkeley: University of California Press, 1990). It was originally written for a doctorate that could never be completed due to ill-health.
5. Barthes, *The Fashion System*, x. This book is Barthes's first attempt to analyse the relationship between images and text in the abstract production of Fashion—not clothing nor the mannequins that fashion spawns.
6. I have chosen the word 'feet' as an example because of its peculiar link with the *swadeshi* campaign: In uniting India around the independence agenda, Gandhi was firmly aware that the hierarchical mentality of the Hindu caste system was one of the main reasons why Indians were subjugated by Indians themselves. In promoting *khadi* he wanted to involve people of all castes—even the lowest caste (the 'feet') and those who were considered outcaste (the *Dalit*).
7. W. Shakespeare, *Romeo and Juliet*, II, ii, 1594.
8. F. Saussure, *Course in General Linguistics*, (tr.) Wade Baskin (London: Fontana/Collins, [1916] 1983), 112 cited in David Chandler, *Semiotics: The Basics* (New York: Routledge, 2002), 24.
9. Roland Barthes, *Mythologies* (London : Paladin, 1973), 121.
10. Cf. Barthes, *Mythologies*, 17.
11. To refer to the second order of signification, Barthes called the connoted sign a 'myth'. I have preferred to use the world 'symbol' to distinguish it from the complex meanings that are often associated with the term 'myth' in common parlance, such as 'fictitious', 'invented', 'supernatural' or 'legendary'—each of which carry a specific nuance. Thus, if denotation produces the 'sign', connotation produces the 'myth' or

'symbol'. This variation in terminology, I believe, does not take me away from the Saussurian tradition and Barthes's notion of myth. Saussure avoided referring to linguistic signs as 'symbols' because he admitted that the popular word referred to non-verbal signs that are not wholly arbitrary in their significance, like the pair of scales to signify/symbolise justice. My use of the word 'symbol' is in perfect continuity with Saussure's understanding since this book deals with 'clothing' as a non-verbal, second order signifier. Charles Peirce (1839–1914), the father of American semeiotics, used the term 'symbol' to indicate 'a sign which refers to the object that it denotes by virtue of a law, usually an association of general ideas, which operates to cause the symbol to be interpreted as referring to that object.' (Charles Peirce, *Collected Papers of Charles Sanders Peirce*, (Cambridge: Harvard University Press, 1958), 249. For him, a symbol 'is a conventional sign, or one depending upon habit (acquired or inborn)'. Peirce is close to Barthes's second order of signification except that his meaning overlaps with Barthes's third order of signification as well.

12. Barthes, *Mythologies*, 124.
13. Barthes, *Mythologies*, 117–18.
14. Barthes, *Mythologies*, 147.
15. Cf. Barthes, *Mythologies*, 140.
16. Nehru, *The Discovery of India*, 319.
17. At the height of its power the Empire spanned the whole globe. The sun was always shining on at least one of its numerous colonies. This gave credence to the claim, 'The sun never sets on the British Empire'.
18. Cf. Bernard Cohn, *Colonialism and its Forms of Knowledge, The British in India* (New Jersey: Princeton University Press, 1996), 124–25.
19. Cf. the detailed manifestation of the exotic quality of Indian life and dress covered by British newspapers. Cohn, *Colonialism*, 125–27.
20. 'Although the question of a special uniform was raised several times after the queen expressed interest, the Council of India decided that prescribing a dress uniform would be an undue expense for their officials.' Cohn, *Colonialism*, 127. Later in this chapter I will argue that Gandhi's *khadi* revolution did in fact fulfil the Queen's wishes, although in a way she never expected.
21. The Great Indian Famine, 1876–1878, covered an area of 257,000 square miles (670,000 sq km) and caused distress to a population totalling 58,500,000. See *Imperial Gazetteer of India*, vol. III, published under the authority of His Majesty's Secretary of State for India in Council, Oxford: Clarendon Press, 1907, 488. For detailed studies on the famines of India see: Romesh C. Dutt, *The Economic History of India*, vol. I (London: Kegan Paul, Trench Trübner, 1902); H.C. Srivastava, *The History of Indian Famines from 1858–1918*, (Agra: Sri Ram Mehra and Co., 1968); Amartya Sen, *Poverty and Famines: An Essay on Entitlements and Deprivation*, (Oxford: Clarendon Press, 1982).
22. Gandhi, *Autobiography*, 211.
23. *Achakan*s are men's long-sleeved coat-like garment, worn close-fitted, reaching down to the knees or lower and buttoned in the front-middle.
24. Nehru, *Autobiography*, 212. The occasion was the inauguration of the Benares Hindu University on 16 February 1916.
25. *Ibid.*

26. *Ibid.*

27. Cf. Michael Lange, ed., *Introduction to Structuralism* (New York: Basic, 1970), 4, quoted in Michael Carter, *Fashion Classics from Carlyle to Barthes*, (Oxford: Berg, 2003), 144.

28. The influence of Karl Marx on Barthes's thinking is apparent in many of his writings, as for instance in *Mythologies*. His aim is to show how this basic economic model is at the root of socio-cultural meaning.

29. Cf. Barthes, *The Fashion System*, 145–46.

30. Barthes, *The Fashion System*, 6.

31. Cf. Barthes, *The Fashion System*, x. Emphasis added. Barthes writes with a double purpose: to explain the fashion system, and to refine an extra-linguistic system of analysis as such.

32. Cf. Barthes, *The Fashion System*, x –xi.

33. Barthes, *The Fashion System*, xi.

34. Barthes, *The Fashion System*, 3.

35. Cf. Barthes, *The Fashion System*, 4.

36. Cf. Barthes, *The Fashion System*, 3.

37. Cf. Barthes, *The Fashion System*, 4–5.

38. Cf. Barthes, *The Fashion System*, 5.

39. Barthes, *The Fashion System*, 8 .

40. Barthes, *The Fashion System*, xi.

41. Cf. *ibid.*

42. Cf. Roland Barthes, 'Histoire et sociologie du vêtement: Quelques observations méthodologiques,' *Annales* (July–September 1957 published in *Œuvres Complètes*, vol. 1, Paris, Seuil, 1993, 744. Our study is based on the review of this work by Carter, *Fashion Classics*, 154.

43. Barthes, *The Fashion System*, 17.

44. Barthes, *The Fashion System*, 10.

45. Cf. Carter, *Fashion Classics*, 154. Kress explains how the used garment cannot escape the constraints of cultural conventions. 'Both dressing according to a code and by dressing in contravention of a code I am constrained by the code. The kinds of items of clothing available in any one time in any one culture, even when I combine them in "impermissible" or "creative" ways, still constitute the limits of what I can construct by way of a message.' G. Kress, *Communication and Culture: An introduction* (Kensington: New South Wales University Press, 1988), 15.

46. Cf. Carter, *Fashion Classics*, 149.

47. Nehru, *The Discovery of India*, 316.

48. John Forbes Watson, *The Textile Manufactures and Costumes of the People of India* (London: G.E. Eyre & W. Spottiswoode, 1866), 5; in Cohn, *Colonialism*, 145.

49. Watson, *The Textile Manufactures*, 2–3, in Emma Tarlo, *Clothing Matters, Dress and Identity in India* (Chicago: University of Chicago Press, 1996), 40. [Emphasis Watson's.]

50. Watson, *The Textile Manufactures*, 8, in Cohn, *Colonialism*, 146.

51. See Bipin Chandra, 'Reinterpretations of Nineteenth Century Indian Economic History', *Indian Economic and Social History Review* (1968), 5:55.

52. See the illustration entitled, 'The Baboo's Progress or What we are coming to!' from *The Indian Charivari*, 7 March 1873, 136.

53. N.C. Chaudhuri, *Culture in the Vanity Bag: Clothing and Adornment in Passing and Abiding India* (Bombay: Jaico Publishing House, 1976), 58, cited in Cohn, *Colonialism*, 132.

54. Cohn, *Colonialism*, 134.

55. Examples of such treatises are: Thomas Williamson, *East-India Vade Mecum* (1810); James Johnson, *The Influence of Tropical Climates* (1813); J.B. Gilchrist, *The General East India Guide and Vade Mecum* (1825); John McCosh, *Medical Advice to the Indian Stranger* (1841); Dr Julius Jefferies, *The British Army in India: Its Preservation by an Appropriate Clothing* (1858). Dr Jefferies was also the inventor of the sola *topi*. James Forbes Watson, *The Textile Manufactures and the Costumes of the People of India* (1866); W. J. Moore, *The Manual of Family Medicine for India* (1883).

56. Cf. Thomas Williamson, *The East-India Vade Mecum* (London: Black, Parry & Kingsbury, 1810), 9, in Cohn, *Colonialism*, 150.

57. Cf. John B. Gilchrist, *The General East India Guide and Vade Mecum* (London: Kingsbury, Parbury, & Allen, 1825), 526–27, in Cohn, *Colonialism*, 151.

58. John McCosh, *Medical Advice to the Indian Stranger*, 79, in Cohn, *Colonialism*, 153.

59. Johnson, *The Influence of Tropical Climate*, 421–22, in Cohn, *Colonialism*, 156.

60. Cohn, *Colonialism*, 155.

61. The complete quote is: 'Only their insularity and unimaginativeness have made the English retain the English style (of dress) in India, even though they admit that it is most uncomfortable for this Indian climate.' *CWMG*, 251.

62. 'Appropriate' for Gandhi meant 'non-violent' and 'egalitarian' options.

63. Barthes, *The Fashion System*, 10.

64. Susan Bean, 'Gandhi and Khadi, Fabric of Independence,' in *Cloth and Human Experience*, eds Annette Weiner and Jane Schneider (Washington: Smithsonian Books, 1989), 365.

65. See, for example, Gandhi, *Autobiography*, 108. He appears in faultless English dress before the Station Master so that he does not suffer the humiliation of being refused a first-class ticket. In this episode, Gandhi's intentional and ostentatious use of English dress to his own advantage reveals his comprehension of the political significance of clothing.

66. Nehru, *The Discovery of India*, 392.

67. Prabhu and Rao, *MMG*, 406–07.

3

Turner: Social Drama in Gandhi's Swadeshi Revolution

The performance is often a critique, direct or veiled, of the social life it grows out of, an evaluation (with lively possibilities of rejection) of the way society handles history.[1]

Victor Turner

The semiological analysis of signs taken up in our previous chapter is a valid and enriching interpretation of our theme. Meanings can be studied as items in neat boxes positioned at three different levels of profundity. Yet this analysis is insufficient because it dissects the structure and meaning of signs in a synchronous or frozen time-frame. Real life is *diachronic*. It is a continuous evolution of varied processes that shift the parameters of semiotic attributes. Meanings are constantly assumed, appropriated, reconstructed, consumed and surrendered within the complexity of evolving spaces of time and context. Meanings are forever integrated within the socio-cultural processes of life and activity. The semiotic study on the sartorial symbolisation of the Indian Independence Movement, therefore, needs a complementary paradigm—one that looks at the *process of signification*, one that investigates the evolutionary construction of meaning, not merely as fixed and isolated categories, but as an integral part of anthropological and historical transformation.

The Anthropology of Performance of Victor Turner (1920–1983) is pertinent to our need for a diachronic communication analysis of the Gandhian Swadeshi Movement. A renowned cultural anthropologist, Turner did extensive comparative research on the symbolism of conflict and crisis resolution. With his PhD on the Ndembu tribe of Zambia he created his own style of ethnographic research. Basically eclectic in his approach, he used ideas developed by others to enlighten and enrich his ethnographic findings. He is recognised as a path breaker in the still evolving communication science called 'Performance Theory'.

Throughout his research, Turner concentrated on performative symbolisation in human rituals. He analysed how rites shaped organisations, actors, relationships and modes of communication in the process of negotiating social change. In the late 1970s he was drawn to theatre and worked closely with theatre artist and one of the founders of Performance Studies, Richard Schechner (1934–present). This collaboration heightened his awareness of the power of symbols in human communication and the 'theatrical' potential in social life. It led him to invent a new term to describe and analyse social change. He called it 'social drama'.[2]

Comparative symbology

Turner's aim as a cultural anthropologist was to study symbols, that is, the second order of signification dealt with in Chapter 2, not in abstraction from human social activity, but as involved in socio-psychological processes.[3] This science he called 'comparative symbology'. It differs from the science of semiotics or semiology insofar as the latter 'eliminates diachronic elements' and studies signs 'as a state of the system, a cross section of history'.[4] Comparative symbology instead is embedded in fieldwork and analyses of symbols within time frames, both in relation to other symbols as well as in their impact with all actors involved.[5] According to Turner:

> Symbols [...] are crucially involved in situations of societal change—the symbol becomes associated with human interests, purposes, ends and means, aspirations and ideals, individual and collective, whether these are explicitly formulated or have to be inferred from the observed behavior [...] I want to stress here that because from the very outset I formulate symbols as social and cultural dynamic systems, shedding and gathering meaning over time and altering in form, I cannot regard them merely as 'terms' in atemporal, logical or protological cognitive systems.[6]

Symbols thus viewed are:

> [...] dynamic semantic systems gaining and losing meanings—and meaning in a social context always has emotional and volitional dimensions—as

they 'travel through' a *single* rite or work of art, let alone through centuries of performance and are aimed at production effect on the psychological states and behaviour to those exposed to them or obliged to use them for their communication with other human beings. I have always tried to link my work in processual analysis [...] with my work in the analysis of ritual performances.[7]

Turner wants to open up the significance of signs and symbols to the flow of multiple meanings that they tend to acquire in the course of human interaction. A fixed, static, formal, cognitive analysis based on arbitrariness (such as between Saussure's signified and signifier) or binary divisions (such as the structuralists' opposites: thin–fat, rich–poor, happy–sad, and so on) may seem useful to qualify and generate meaning[8] but suffer from simplifying their interpretation within real contexts. The place where symbols flourish is not in some idealised figment of the semiotician's imagination but in the actual world which is a 'forest of symbols' that is a complex, continuously changing milieu. Both as signifiers (perceivable forms) or as signifieds (meanings), signs and symbols are involved in a multiple variability. This cannot be otherwise because they are created by human beings 'living, conscious, emotional and volitional creatures who employ them not only to give order to the universe they inhabit, but creatively to make use also of disorder.'[9]

Structural semiotics is often too entrenched in textual analysis to investigate how people in everyday life achieve order through constructing texts. It does not explain processes of production, audience interpretation or authorial intentions. It ignores the milieu that is laden with frameworks that condition popular interpretation of culture, economy and politics as well as the tendency to favour agendas that are promoted by institutional, conservative and dominant groups.[10] In short, Turner wishes to bring the reader into the midst of the group experience of symbol-making:

Comparative symbology does attempt to preserve this ludic capacity, to catch symbols in their movement, so to speak, and to 'play' with their possibilities of form and meaning. It does this by contextualising symbols in the concrete, historical fields of their use by 'men alive' as they act, react, transact and interact socially.[11]

As examples of progressive symbolisation in the Swadeshi Movement I refer briefly to three instances.

The conflicting hermeneutics at play in the designing of the Indian Flag from 1921 to 1947 makes an interesting example of comparative symbology. Gandhi was so convinced about the uniting potential of the *charkha* and *khadi* that he wanted the national flag to epitomise it. The colours chosen, white, green and red, were to represent the diverse faiths and their placement was to signify tolerance and the spirit of the accommodation. 'The weakest [symbolised by the colour white] numerically occupy the first place, the Islamic colour [green] comes next, the Hindu colour red comes last, the idea being that the strongest should act as a shield to the weakest.'[12] In the centre would be placed the spinning-wheel, to 'inform the whole world that we are determined, so far as our food and clothing are concerned, to be totally independent of the rest of it.'[13] Finally, the cloth of the flag had to be made of *khaddar*, 'for it is through coarse cloth alone that we can make India independent of foreign markets for her cloth.'[14]

However, the symbol did not receive unanimous approval. Many were dissatisfied by the religious significance of the flag and the privileges given to different communities. The All India Sanskrit Congress that convened in Calcutta in 1924 preferred the colour saffron to red, and wanted to insert the symbol of the *gadha* (or mace of Lord Vishnu) in the place of the *charkha*. The Sikhs requested that a yellow colour be inserted to represent them. In April 1931, the Congress Working Committee appointed a flag committee to redesign the flag in consideration of the issues raised. Strangely, the committee proposed an all-saffron flag with the *charkha* at upper hoist. The Indian National Congress rejected this single-coloured flag for its communal overtones. Later that year, the Congress met at Karachi and adopted the tricolour flag with a few adjustments. It featured three horizontal strips of saffron on the top, white in the middle and green at the bottom. These were now interpreted as saffron for courage; white for truth and peace; green for faith and prosperity. No communal significance was attributed to the colours. The *charkha* was placed in the centre to symbolise the economic regeneration of India and the industriousness of its people.

As the scheduled day of India's independence approached, the Constituent Assembly was formed to choose, once and for all, the national flag of new India. The committee headed by Rajendra Prasad met on 23 June and reached a decision by 14 July. It resolved that the flag should be acceptable to all parties and that it should not have any communal undertones. The members chose the tricolour of the Congress with one last modification: the spinning wheel was to be replaced by the *Dharma Chakra*, or the Wheel of Righteousness, taken from the pillar of the 3rd Century BC Emperor, Ashoka, the great promoter of peace. The *khadi* flag was unfurled for the first time on 15 August 1947.

Another example of dynamic symbolisation is Gandhi's use of the daily 'spinning franchise' to replace the payment of four *anna*s as Congress membership fee.[15] On the strength of our thesis it would seem that, in rejecting Gandhi's desire to make symbols speak louder than words, the protesting Congress members missed an important opportunity to bridge the great divide between the elite and the poor. In this bridge-building, the first move had to be made by the elite who would have to stoop low to be trustworthy in the eyes of their poverty-stricken brothers and sisters. The 'commitment to spinning' would therefore have been a perfect sign of empathy through which the Congress could enter into dialogue with the rural masses. Apart from the humbling spiritualising character of the exercise (which Gandhi often referred to in his writings) it would have shown that they, the elite Congressmen, had earned their position as leaders of their impoverished people. Credibility was at the heart of the exercise. It had to be a dynamic effortful symbol of solidarity or not at all.

A third study in comparative symbolisation is the difference in the perspectives of B.R. Ambedkar, M.A. Jinnah and V.D. Savarkar on Gandhi's proposal to adopt *khadi* attire as the symbol of Indian identity-in-unity. For Ambedkar, *khadi* was a symbol of retrogression to a past of oppressive Hindu customs from which he strove to liberate his people.[16] For Jinnah, *khadi* was a symbol of the uneducated masses with whom he did not wish to be personally and professionally associated.[17] For Savarkar, *khadi* was impotent and all-embracing: it did not support his struggle for an exclusive Hindu Nation.[18] These different readings of the symbology of *khadi* led the three leaders to take positions that were vehemently opposed to Gandhi's Swadeshi Movement.

Social Drama and the Rites of Passage to Indian Independence

In large-scale societies symbols are created through socio-cultural change, or what Turner calls 'social drama':[19]

When I say that a social drama is 'processually structured,' I mean that it exhibits a regular course of events which can be grouped in successive phases of public action. These are (1) *breach* of regular norm-governed social relations made publicly visible by the infraction of a rule ordinarily held to be binding, and which is itself a symbol of the maintenance of some major relationship between persons, statuses or subgroups held to be a key link in the integrality of the widest community recognised to be a cultural envelope of solidary sentiments; this course of events moves on to the second phase (2) of *crisis*, when people take sides, or rather, are in the process of being induced, seduced, cajoled, nudged or threatened to take sides by those who confront one another across the revealed breach as prime antagonists [...] [the crisis] challenges the representatives of order to grapple with it. Their response inaugurates the third phase, (3) *the application of redressive or remedial procedures*. These range from personal advice and informal mediation or arbitration to formal jural and legal machinery and, to resolve certain kinds of crises or legitimate other modes of conflict-resolution, to the performance of public ritual [...]. The fourth phase (4) of the social drama consists either of the *reintegration* of the disturbed social group, or of the *recognition and legitimation of irreparable schism* between the contending parties.[20]

A diagrammatic overview (Figure 3.1) will help to clarify the application of Turner's social drama to the struggle for Indian Independence.

The four successive phases of public action in the social drama for Indian Independence—breach, crisis, redressive or remedial procedures and reintegration or schism—will now be dealt with separately.

The breach

The breach is the first step in the social drama. It is a demarcation of a separate space and time. It generates symbols of inversion manifested through behaviour, relationships, events and everyday things. These represent the detachment of the 'ritual subjects' or participants of change from the previous ways of thinking and acting.[21]

During the Indian freedom struggle Gandhi made profuse use of symbolic inversions to heighten awareness of the breach that was effected in himself, his volunteers, the Congress, the Indian masses and the British Empire. His change in dress, simplicity of lifestyle, the *bramacharya* vow, the commitment to justice and empowerment of the poor, are different moments in a personal rite of passage. In the eyes of the masses

Figure 3.1: The 'Social Drama' of Indian Independence

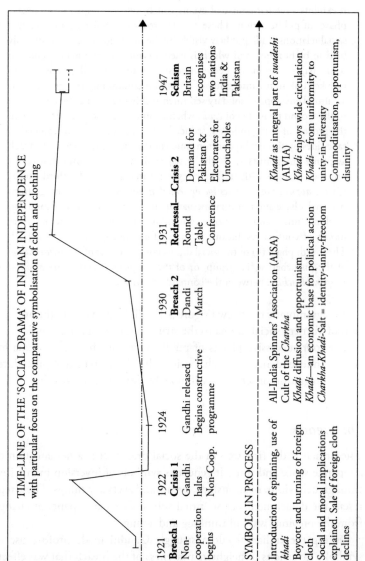

TIME-LINE OF THE 'SOCIAL DRAMA' OF INDIAN INDEPENDENCE
with particular focus on the comparative symbolisation of cloth and clothing

1921	1922	1924	1930	1931	1947
Breach 1	**Crisis 1**		**Breach 2**	**Redressal—Crisis 2**	**Schism**
Non-cooperation begins	Gandhi halts Non-Coop.	Gandhi released Begins constructive programme	Dandi March	Round Table Conference	Britain recognises two nations India & Pakistan
				Demand for Pakistan & Electorates for Untouchables	

SYMBOLS IN PROCESS

Introduction of spinning, use of *khadi*	All-India Spinners' Association (AISA)
Boycott and burning of foreign cloth	Cult of the *Charkha*
Social and moral implications explained. Sale of foreign cloth declines	*Khadi* diffusion and opportunism
	Khadi—an economic base for political action
	Charkha-Khadi-Salt = identity-unity-freedom

Khadi as integral part of *swadeshi* (AIVIA)
Khadi enjoys wide circulation
Khadi—from uniformity to unity-in-diversity
Commoditisation, opportunism, disunity

Source: Author.

these choices transformed him from a South Africa-returned, England-educated lawyer to the Mahatma they had been waiting for.

The breach had strong social dimensions as well, although different from the types of breach listed by Turner. Gandhi's breach was *non-violent*. He was in constant and amicable contact with the authorities he was fighting. Second, the conflict was infused with a *spiritual and moral* conviction that was so powerful that it enabled the ritual subjects to voluntarily suffer the violence of the authority they were opposing. They were ready to sacrifice self and family in order to break away from a subjugated past.[22] Third, Gandhi's breach was not merely directed against British imperialism. It was also *self-directed*. Every participant in the struggle had to confront the enemies within: his own fear, his hatred for the opposing party and his temptation for an armed rebellion.

Gandhi sought to tie the social drama to the personal drama in a way that would be a testimony to the entire world. For him the political was not merely personal, it was also spiritual, moral and, from our perspective, pre-eminently sartorial. The breach had to begin within the soul, but it also had to be seen in public places. These demonstrations were needed to reinforce the unity of the participants in their shared option for truth-force. The breach was *satyagraha*, the yearning for truth, that is, every participant's inner break from mediocrity and injustice. It was a call to *live* a radically different life with the change manifested in the way one dressed. The insistence on spinning, the boycott and burning of foreign cloth, the importance of *khadi* attire, the Gandhi *topi*, the renunciation of government jobs, titles and favours—all these were symbols through which Gandhi called his countrymen and women to a psycho-cultural and spatio-temporal separateness from previous lifestyles under imperial control.

The crisis

The crisis that follows the breach is the *limen* or threshold, the area that Turner calls the 'betwixt and between'.[23] It is a stage experienced by the ritual subjects after they have assertively and symbolically affected the breach. Some of the characteristics of this stage are a feeling of ambiguity and indeterminacy, of being neither here nor there, an experience of limbo or the twilight zone.

The crisis phase in the struggle for Indian independence began when Gandhi brought non-cooperation to a sudden halt on hearing of the Chauri Chaura massacre.[24] Not all who participated in the Non-cooperation Movement understood the full implications of non-violence as an unconditional prerequisite for participating. Gandhi, on the other hand, realised that he had overestimated the capacity of the masses to resist repression without retaliation.[25] This decision caused great confusion in the minds of Congress leaders themselves, let alone the masses.[26] C.F. Andrews describes the all-pervasive disappointment that had gripped the people:

> The immediate consequence of this act of Mahatma Gandhi [halting the Non-cooperation Campaign] was profound dismay [...]. There was a depression all over the country which could everywhere be felt. When I went in and out of the villages at this time, I found that the discouragement had penetrated the country as well as the cities. It was at this moment, as I have related, that the government of India struck its blow. On the charge that certain articles published in Young India had caused disaffection, Mahatma Gandhi was arrested.[27]

B.R. Nanda dedicates four chapters[28] to the crisis that followed Gandhi's arrest and continued even after his release. He mentions the disunity, the lack of enthusiasm and the people's loss of faith in their ability to rise to the great challenge they had initiated. He describes the split in the Congress leadership, the resignation of members from the working committee. He recalls how Gandhi, prematurely released from prison due to an appendicitis operation, was quick to perceive the depth of the crisis: the non-cooperators were non-cooperating not so much with the government but with each other; Hindu–Muslim unity had gone to pieces; mutual suspicion and fear prevailed; the Constructive Programme that sought to raise the social cohesiveness of the people was being scoffed at; the cause of the untouchables was ignored. By 1928 there was a further split in the Congress between those who sought Dominion Status under the British Empire and those who wanted complete independence from the British.[29] Signs of discontent were also visible among industrial workers, peasants and middle-class youth. A number of strikes took place at the textile mills of Bombay, the jute mills of Bengal and the iron and steel works of Jamshedpur. Among the many youth leagues that sprang up around the country militant solutions for political and social redressal were being discussed.[30]

The crisis also had repercussions on decisions regarding the manufacture of cloth and clothing. The enthusiasm for boycotting foreign cloth had subsided. Gandhi sensed the cynicism in his colleagues whenever he mentioned the spinning programme.[31] Some saw the confusion as a direct result of the Non-cooperation Movement and blamed Gandhi for having played on the sentiments of the masses and for having roused them prematurely.[32]

From the morass of doubt and perplexity, Gandhi sought a way out by redeeming the process of symbolisation he had so painstakingly construed. He undertook a fast for unity, inviting all to join him in self-purification 'because the strength of the soul grows in proportion as you subdue the flesh'.[33] With his leadership acumen he was quick to recognise the need for a change of strategy. The new site for remedial action had to be away from politics and far from the cities. It had to involve millions of simple villagers. It had to begin from the bottom. For the next three years he concentrated his efforts on the implementation of the Constructive Programme through volunteers. The spinning wheel and untouchability were dominant themes during this period. He established the All India Spinners' Association (AISA) with the primary objective of making employment available to as many rural people as possible, thus drawing greater numbers into the *swadeshi* campaign. The *charkha* became more than a political, anti-imperial symbol that replaced foreign cloth. It was now a vision of a peaceful, non-exploitative and self-sustainable life.[34]

In this moment of crisis, it is worth noting how a complex Indian society sought to reinterpret Gandhi's sartorial symbolism. The significance of *khadi* began to be tailored to people's interests. Western educated Indians, including loyal Congressmen wondered whether the *khadi* cult was not being overdone. Complaints came in against *khadi* as unsuitable for modern living: it would not stand the wear and tear of factory work; it was too thick and heavy and was hard to launder; it was unsuitable for women and children.[35] People in cities and towns wanted finer *khadi* in beautiful designs and colours and production and marketing began to cater to their wishes.[36] *Khadi* dress, originally intended to eliminate distinctions, began to manifest signs of class, gender and religious identity.[37] Some mill owners profiteered by adulterating the original symbol with their mill-made variety. The unitary and performative impact of Gandhi's symbolisation was starting to stretch beyond his expectations and control, sometimes compromising the very principles of *purna swaraj*.[38]

The British Government considered Gandhi's switch from politics to social work just another new obsession.[39] Only in 1930, when it became evident that the *khadi* campaign was a part of a larger political struggle against the Empire, did the Government wake up to the consequences of Gandhi's symbolisation. But by then it was far too late to stop the rivers of men and women in white *khadi* walking courageously to manufacture salt at Dandi on 6 April 1930. Moreover, salt, a new symbol of freedom from the English yoke, was born.

Redressive or remedial procedures

Turner's third phase in the social drama is the application of redressive or remedial procedures. It is the most reflexive of the three stages. 'The community, acting through its representatives, bends, even throws itself back upon itself, to measure what some of its members have done, and how they have conducted themselves with reference to its own standards.'[40] This stage could also be marked by violence or could lead to a further revolution that begins 'an extended social drama on the scale of a nation'.[41] A solidarity around core values begins to dominate. It provokes a type of plural self-scrutiny, where antecedent events are assessed in the light of reason. Animosities of the community in crisis are at times expressed through symbols of sacrifice and heroism.[42]

Some redressive and remedial features that followed the crisis that climaxed in the second breach of the Dandi March are: the First Round Table Conference, the Gandhi–Irwin Pact and the Second Round Table Conference. These positive signs were interspersed with other non-remedial measures. Following Lord Irwin's departure for England, the Indian National Congress was outlawed. There was a new turn to the social drama with the rise in communal politics. The two-nation theory propagated by Jinnah began to gain popularity among Muslims.[43] Ambedkar sought separate electorates for the untouchables but had to compromise his stand, in deference to Gandhi's fast.[44]

Through this maze of political self-reflection now divided across political and communal lines, the instances of compromise and abuse detected at the crisis phase became more evident. Among some groups, Gandhi's sartorial symbolisation experienced further deviations. Differences in attire that reflected religious, regional, cultural and caste identities were stubbornly maintained.[45] Caste Hindus protested against the sale of *khadi* produced by untouchables beyond the confines of their own communities.[46] Similarly, Hindus refused to use *khadi* made by Muslim weavers.[47] The sacredness of the symbol was now no guarantee of the sacredness of the wearer. The pervasive use of *khadi* psychologically coerced even those who did not believe in its moral signification to conform out of sheer human respect. When social and political leaders took to wearing *khadi* merely for its popularity and the moral ascendancy it had over the masses, the symbol that was once sacred became a sign of hypocrisy. *Khadi* began to be used as a mask to conceal one's dubious intentions.[48]

This negative turn to the symbolism of *khadi* was compounded by the contamination of the symbol itself. It happened when greedy mill owners began to produce imitation *khadi* and to sell it at cheaper rates through Congress outlets in cities, thus undercutting the rural poor and depriving them of a sizeable income. Gandhi's original construction of meaning had been usurped by the unscrupulous who were prepared to tarnish for their private gain the integrity and dedication of all Indians, especially the vast village population.[49]

Reintegration or recognition of irreparable schism

The fourth and final stage in Turner's social drama is the reintegration or legitimation of irreparable schism. It consists of actions that restore peace and acceptance of differences. Parties agree to disagree. They decide to live in tolerance and understanding of differences. Yet, this happens only when social dramas are complete. Turner says that dramas of major social change may not complete the course but may instead revert to further crisis.[50]

In the Indian social drama for independence the resolution and recognition of schism came in two instances—the granting of independence to India, with the simultaneous creation of a new independent nation for Muslims called East and West Pakistan. While the schism between India and Britain was smooth, that of India and Pakistan was bloody.

The manipulative tendencies of certain sections of the population which were corrupting the very purpose underlying *khadi* manufacture forced Gandhi to think of alternatives. A shift from a city-centred marketing strategy was needed. He began to see *khadi* promotion as an integral part of a holistic village development plan.[51] Thus, from 1935, the concept of *khadi* work underwent a radical change. The emphasis was placed on *samagra seva* or all-round service. *Khadi* work became part of village life. It included all the processes: from picking cotton to slivering and from production to consumption. Even as the Government's repression continued to undermine AISA's network, greater efforts were made to promote the *charkha* in every village home so that it was plied not merely for earning wages but also for the ultimate aim of making village India self-sufficient in all her requirements. Village reconstruction came to be seen as a comprehensive socio-symbolic process that embraced all aspects of village life.[52]

As independence drew near, people began to look retrospectively at the 30 years of struggle and the symbolic role played by cloth and clothing in uniting them. *Khadi* began to be exalted as the 'livery of freedom' and was made the obligatory fabric of the National Flag.

Liminality and Communitas

Underlying the 'social drama' are two important concepts that are particularly important to our study of the use of symbols during the Swadeshi Movement. Turner calls them 'Liminality' and 'Communitas'. Although his initial source for arriving at such concepts was the Ndembu tribal culture, it is worth noting that he widened his research base among sophisticated industrial societies as well. In doing so he confirmed his initial findings in a variety of social contexts and thereby validated their applicability:

> Liminal entities are neither here nor there; they are betwixt and between the positions assigned and arrayed by law, custom, convention, and ceremonial. As such their ambiguous and indeterminate attributes are expressed by a rich variety of symbols in the many societies that ritualize social and cultural transitions. Thus, liminality is frequently likened to death, to being in the womb, to invisibility, to darkness, to bisexuality, to the wilderness, and to an eclipse of the sun and the moon.[53]

Gandhi's Swadeshi Movement and the period from 1921 to 1947 during which it was in operation was truly a liminal spatio-temporal event. It was a period of transition when the country, having committed

the breach, was neither dependent on nor independent of British imperialism. Participants in the *swadeshi* campaign suffered a long experience
of Turner's 'betwixt and between'. This was certainly one of the most
creative moments in the history of the country; a period charged with
affective and participatory symbolism realised through group events,
actions, gestures, behaviours, dressing, work, processions, memorials,
anniversaries, conferences, conventions, social work, volunteering, appeals, dramas, publications, prayers, scriptural reinterpretations, sacrificial signs, fasts, and at the core of it all, a charismatic leader who symbolised in his own person the liminality of his people. Turner's research on
liminal persons (or neophytes) unequivocally replicates the experience
of participants in the campaign:

> Liminal entities, such as neophytes in initiation or puberty rites, may be
> represented as possessing nothing. They may be disguised as monsters,
> wear only a strip of clothing, or even go naked, to demonstrate that as
> liminal beings they have no status, property, insignia, secular clothing
> indicating rank or role, position in a kinship system—in short, noth-
> ing that may distinguish them from their fellow neophytes or initiands.
> Their behavior is normally passive or humble; they must obey their in-
> structors implicitly, and accept arbitrary punishment without complaint.
> It is as though they are being reduced or ground down to a uniform
> condition to be fashioned anew and endowed with additional powers to
> enable them to cope with their new station in life. Among themselves,
> neophytes tend to develop an intense comradeship and egalitarianism.
> Secular distinctions of rank and status disappear or are homogenized.[54]

The reference to obedience must be seen in the right perspective when
applying the concept of liminality to the *satyagraha* struggle. It appears
paradoxical yet true. The obedience of the civilly disobedient *satyagrahi*s
was their fundamental submission to the laws of the colonisers. They
disobeyed the unjust laws, but allowed the judicial law to take its course.
Obedience (that is, courting arrest) was the underlying consequence
of disobedience (to an unjust law). Gandhi's confession before Judge
Broomfield after the Chauri Chaura massacre is a remarkable example
of such obedience of the civilly disobedient *satyagrahi*:

> I had to make my choice. I had either to submit to a system which, I
> considered has done an irreparable harm to my country or incur the risk
> of the mad fury of my people bursting forth when they understood the
> truth from my lips. I know that my people have sometimes gone mad.

I am deeply sorry for it; and I am, therefore, here to submit not to a light penalty but to the highest penalty. I do not ask for mercy. I do not plead any extenuating act [...]. The only course open to you, Mr Judge is [...] either to resign your post or inflict on me the severest penalty if you believe that the system and law you are assisting to administer are good for the people.[55]

This incident also serves to introduce Turner's dual model of interrelatedness elaborated in his work, *The Ritual Process*.[56] Table 3.1 highlights the two conflicting aspects in any social drama, namely, the structure-anti-structure dichotomy. The anti-structure is the liminal experience which he calls 'communitas'. The name he gives emphasises 'modality of social relationship' rather than an 'area of common living'.[57] He also calls the structure the 'status-system'.[58]

It is interesting to observe the perfect correspondence, first, between Turner's theoretical list on communitas and the concrete experience shared by Gandhi's *satyagrahis* during the *swadeshi* campaign and, second, between Turner's descriptive list on formal structure and the well-established system of Imperial Government control. The strong affinity of the properties of communitas with characteristics upheld by many religious traditions is also striking. Turner explains why this is so. The manifold symbols through which the above properties are manifested and embodied 'often relate to the physiological processes of death and birth, anabolism and katabolism.'[59] The progressive complexity of modern societies has led to the increasing specialisation and division of labour in the form of religion from a set of transitional qualities in tribal societies.

This insight of Turner's cultural anthropology brings to light the role played by religion in the symbolisation of the struggle for *swaraj*. Gandhi proposed the personal act of spinning as a disciplinary and spiritual exercise, a ritual sacrifice (*yajna*) that had to be accepted in true sincerity by all participants in the struggle—from Congress members to the poorest in the villages.[60]

The production of *khadi* was also a way of purging out foreign cloth, a symbol of British domination and evil. The public boycott and bonfires of foreign cloth were considered virtues. They were powerful visual representations of *yajna* and self-purification by fire—a potent symbol in Hindu sacrificial rites. The purification expressed by the burning of foreign cloth was not meant to be directed against the cloth itself, nor the English people who produced it. The purification was from the sin of complicity

Table 3.1: Communitas and Structure

Communitas (Satyagraha volunteers)	Structure (British Empire)
Transition	State
Totality	Partiality
Homogeneity	Heterogeneity
Equality	Inequality
Anonymity	Systems of nomenclature
Absence of property	Property
Absence of status	Status
Nakedness or uniform clothing	Distinctions of clothing
Sexual continence	Sexuality
Minimisation of sex distinctions	Maximisation of sex distinctions
Absence of rank	Distinctions of rank
Humility	Just pride of position
Disregard for personal appearance	Care for personal appearance
No distinctions of wealth	Distinctions of wealth
Unselfishness	Selfishness
Total obedience	Obedience only to the superior rank
Sacredness	Secularity
Sacred instruction	Technical knowledge
Silence	Speech
Suspension of kinship rights and obligations	Kinship rights and obligations
Continuous reference to mystical powers	Intermittent reference to mystical powers
Foolishness	Sagacity
Simplicity	Complexity
Acceptance of pain and suffering	Avoidance of pain and suffering
Heteronomy	Degrees of autonomy

Source: Peter Gonsalves, based on the 'structure and anti-structure' paradigm by Victor Turner, *The Ritual Process—Structure and Anti-structure,* New York, Aldine de Gruyter, 1969 (1997), 106–07.

in one's dependence on foreign cloth while foregoing one's own dignity and duty to produce it. The sin from which the Indian people had to be purified was their willingness to shamefully bow down to British imperialism.[61] 'In burning my foreign cloths, I burn my shame.'[62]

The political and spiritual breach was to be represented outwardly through *khadi* attire—the investiture of goodness. Wearing *khadi* carried with it the moral imperative of living by *dharma* (duty), living out the '*khadi* spirit'.[63] Giving up the use of foreign cloth and clothing was 'like changing one's religion'[64]—a transformation in one's morals, spirituality and beliefs. Gandhi's own personal example of shifting to the single-piece loincloth[65] in 1921 set him apart as a saint-politician ready to practise what he preached, ready even to identify with the poorest in order to be their representative before the world. Gandhi's approach was holistic: 'Politics divorced from religion have absolutely no meaning'[66] because '[h]uman life being an undivided whole, no line could ever be drawn between its different compartments, nor between ethics and politics'.[67]

In conclusion, I present Gandhi's own view on 'the betwixt and between'. In a strikingly down-to-earth passage published in his first major work, he reveals a perfect awareness of the notion of liminality long before Turner articulated it. He even acknowledges the healthy role liminality plays in evolution and progress:

> When a man rises from sleep, he twists his limbs and is restless. It takes some time before he is entirely awakened. Similarly, although the Partition has caused an awakening, the comatose state has not yet disappeared. We are still twisting our limbs and still restless, and just as the state between sleep and awakening must be considered to be necessary, so may the present unrest in India a necessary and, therefore, a proper state. The knowledge that there is unrest will, it is highly probable, enable us to outgrow it [...]. Unrest is in reality discontent [...]. This discontent is a very useful thing. So long as a man is contented with his present lot, so long is it difficult to persuade him to come out of it. Therefore it is that every reform must be preceded by discontent [...]. All these may be considered as good signs, but they may also lead to bad results.[68]

In order to harness the forces of unrest as a power for good, Gandhi understood the importance of a symbol to define his people's socio-political identity; to maintain unity in their complex diversity; to provide a vision towards which all could orientate their physical, psychological and spiritual energies; to build unswerving commitment and daily perseverance in the face of temptations to look back or to stray.

His symbol had to motivate and maintain the courage they needed to sacrifice their lives for a cause. It had to be a sign of his people's own collective achievement, a work of their hands. It had to be the basis for a belief in their capacity for independence. It had to be a reminder of the high ideal towards which they were progressively striving: nothing less than *purna swaraj*.

So Gandhi chose *khadi*. It was the symbol of his prescient dream for India—that of bringing together the diverse strands of his people in order to spin a durable yarn from which future leaders would weave the fabric of an independent and multicoloured nation.

Notes

1. Victor Turner, *The Anthropology of Performance* (New York: Performing Arts Journal Publications, 1988), 22.
2. Victor Turner, *From Ritual to Theatre* (New York: Performing Arts Journal Publications, 1982), 9.
3. Cf. *ibid*, 21.
4. Roland Barthes, *Elements of Semiology* (London: Jonathan Cape, 1967), 98, cited in Turner, *From Ritual to Theatre*, 21.
5. Cf. Turner, *From Ritual to Theatre*, 21.
6. Turner, *From Ritual to Theatre*, 22.
7. *Ibid.*
8. Cf. Chandler, *Semiotics*, 104.
9. Turner, *From Ritual to Theatre*, 23.
10. Cf. Chandler, *Semiotics*, 210.
11. Turner, *From Ritual to Theatre*, 23.
12. *CWMG*, vol. 19, 34–35.
13. *Ibid.*
14. *Ibid.*
15. Cf. *CWMG*, vol. 25, 349–50.
16. See. B.R. Ambedkar, 'Waiting for a Visa,' in *Writings and Speeches*, Vasant Moon ed., vol. 12 (Bombay: Education Department, Government of Maharashtra, 1993), Part I, 661–91, web version Columbia University: http://www.columbia.edu/itc/mealac/pritchett/00ambedkar/txt_ambedkar_waiting.html (6 April 2007).
17. From the very beginning, Jinnah's sartorial preference contrasts strongly with Gandhi's. On arriving in England for his studies, four years after Gandhi, 'Jinnah [...] lost no time in casting off his traditional Kathiawari coat and turban and switching to smart suits. Jinnah's transformation was not merely sartorial; his Anglicism, unlike Gandhi's, was uninhibited and total; till the end of his life he kept up the lifestyle of an upper-class English gentleman. Before leaving England he even modernised his name by changing "Mohammad Ali Jinnahbhai" to "M.A. Jinnah".' B.R. Nanda, *In Search of Gandhi*, 53.

18. Cf. A.G. Noorani, 'Savarkar and Gandhi,' *Frontline* 20 (15–28 March 2003): 6, http://www.frontlineonnet.com/fl2006/stories/20030328003603400.htm(15 October 2006).

19. Turner developed the 'social drama' concept from Arnold van Gennep's *Rites de Passage* which was first published in French in 1908 to refer to changes in the lives of individuals or groups or seasonal changes for an entire society. The term has come to be used almost exclusively in connection with 'life-crisis' rituals. Van Gennep distinguishes three phases in a rite of passage: separation, transition and incorporation. Cf. Turner, *From Ritual to Theatre*, 24. Our presentation of 'social drama' is confined to Turner's reinterpretation and use of new terminology.

20. Turner, *From Ritual to Theatre*, 24.

21. Cf. *ibid.*

22. The experience of Nehru sums up the feeling caused by the breach with the past: 'Nineteen twenty-one was an extraordinary year for us. There was a strange mixture of nationalism and politics and religion and mysticism and fanaticism. Behind all this was agrarian trouble and, in the big cities, a rising working-class movement. Nationalism and vague but intense countrywide idealism sought to bring together all these various, and sometimes mutually contradictory discontents, and succeeded to a remarkable degree [...]. Even more remarkable was the fact that these desires and passions were relatively free from hatred of the alien rulers against whom they were directed [...]. It was this extraordinary stiffening-up of the masses that filled us with confidence. A demoralised, backward, and broken-up people suddenly straightened their backs and lifted their heads and took part in disciplined, joint action on a country-wide scale.' Nehru, *Autobiography*, 81–83.

23. Cf. Victor Turner, *The Forest of Symbols* (Ithaca: Cornell University Press, 1986), 93–111. The chapter is entitled 'Betwixt and Between: The Liminal Period in Rites de Passage.'

24. The crime took place on 4 February 1922. Gandhi came to know of the incident four days later. On February 10 at Bardoli, he announced his decision to stop the Civil Disobedience Movement immediately. Two days later he began his five-day fast as penance. He was arrested on 11 March.

25. Earlier, in 1919, when violence broke out in Ahmedabad against the Rowlatt Bills, Gandhi called his decision to embark on *satyagraha*—a Himalayan miscalculation because he erroneously believed that the people were principled enough to resist non-violence even at the slightest provocation.

26. 'The sudden suspension of mass civil disobedience shocked and bewildered Gandhi's closest colleagues... [Gandhi's] ardent followers were troubled by doubts and torn between loyalty to their leader and their own convictions.' Cf. Nanda, *Mahatma Gandhi*, 231–32.

27. C.F. Andrews, *Mahatma Gandhi: His Life and Ideas* (Mumbai: Jaico Publishing House, 2005), 211.

28. Cf. Nanda, *Mahatma Gandhi*, 231–68.

29. Cf. Nanda, *In Search of Gandhi*, 76.

30. Cf. *ibid.*

31. Gandhi admitted: 'After all, those who have led an active political life in the old fashion cannot possibly be expected to sit idle, whilst dreamers like me expect to evolve an intensely active programme out of a harmless toy like the spinning-wheel.' Nanda, *Mahatma Gandhi*, 255.

32. Gandhi saw it differently: 'The awakening of the masses was a necessary part of the training. I would do nothing to put the people to sleep again.' Nanda, *Mahatma Gandhi*, 257.

33. Nanda, *Mahatma Gandhi*, 259. On obtaining a promise by leaders of the dissenting communities to work in harmony, Gandhi broke his fast on 8 October 1924.

34. The value of *khadi* produced increased from about Rs. 19 lakhs in 1924–25 to 32 lakhs in 1935 (approximately from $44,186 to $74,418). Cf. Government of India, Publications Division, *The Khadi Industry*, 1962, 7.

35. Addressing these issues, Gandhi urged people to be patient, promising that with more skill better *khadi* would be available. He constantly urged them to look beyond the inconveniences of *khadi* to its symbolic value and the economic benefit for the dispersed masses.

36. Emma Tarlo, *Clothing Matters, Dress and Identity in India* (Chicago: University of Chicago Press, 1996), 105–06.

37. Cf. *CWMG*, vol. 75, 166–67.

38. See Gandhi's opinion on the refined brand of *khadi* in his speech at Devakottah, 24 September 1927, in *CWMG*, vol. 35, 28. Gandhi distinguished between 'fashionable *khadi* wearers' and those who took the '*khadi* vow'. He believed that only the latter could advance the true spirit of *khadi*. *CWMG*, vol. 19, 345–46.

39. Cf. Nanda, *Mahatma Gandhi*, 263.

40. Turner, *The Anthropology of Performance*, 34.

41. *Ibid.*

42. Cf. *ibid.*

43. Cf. Jinnah's speech at the Muslim League Conference in Lahore, 1940.

44. The Poona Pact was signed on 24 September 1932.

45. Generally Hindus wore *dhoti*s, *kurta*s and Gandhi *topi*s, Muslims wore *kurta* pyjamas with a cap or fez, Sikhs retained their turbans. Cf. Bean, *Cloth and Human Experience*, 373.

46. Cf. *CWMG*, vol. 25, 24.

47. Cf. *CWMG*, vol. 24, 426.

48. Cf. *CWMG*, vol. 25, 235; *CWMG*, vol. 28, 143; and *CWMG*, vol. 31, 57.

49. Cf. *CWMG*, vol. 28, 144.

50. Cf. Turner, *The Anthropology of Performance*, 35.

51. One way of dealing with the spurious *khadi* was to increase the wages of spinners. Thus, in 1935 AISA stipulated a fair wage that was higher than private profiteering agencies. With World War II in 1939, the shortage of cloth gave a fillip to the *khadi* industry. It increased from Rs. 24 lakhs worth in 1936 to Rs 134 lakhs in 1944–45. The wages of spinners, weavers and other artisans rose from Rs 17 lakhs to about Rs 75 lakhs. *Khadi* was sold at fixed prices so that even when the price of mill-cloth increased, *khadi* was cheaper. Cf. *The Khadi Industry*, 8. (Rs 1 lakh = Rs 100,000).

52. For a detailed study of the shift in *khadi* policy, cf. Rahul Ramagundam, *Gandhi's Khadi, A History of Contention and Conciliation* (Hyderabad: Orient Longman Private Limited, 2008), 256. Official reports published by the Government of India state that the value of *khadi* produced increased from 71 lakhs in 1945–1946 to more than Rs 127 lakhs in 1950–1951, and the wages distributed to the spinners, weavers and other artisans increased from Rs 52 lakhs to Rs 72 lakhs. Cf. *The Khadi Industry*, 9.

53. Victor Turner, *The Ritual Process—Structure and Anti-structure* (New York: Aldine de Gruyter, 1969), 95.
54. *Ibid.*
55. Nanda, *Mahatma Gandhi*, 240.
56. Cf. Turner, *The Ritual Process*, 106–07.
57. He does not use the word 'community' precisely because the word is often linked to a spatial location. Turner, *The Ritual Process*, 96.
58. Turner, *The Ritual Process*, 106.
59. Turner, *The Ritual Process*, 107.
60. Gandhi took his inspiration for the *yajna* from the *Bhagavad Gita*: 'In doing anything as *yagna*, one is not concerned with the fruit of one's labour and, therefore, the fruit is immeasurable [...] one learns the science and art of working, [...] purity of heart, [...] single-minded devotion [...]. A person who works in the spirit of sacrifice will be a lover of truth....' In S.R. Bakshi, *Gandhi and Ideology of Swadeshi* (New Delhi: Reliance Publishing House, 1987), vi.
61. Cf. *ibid.*, 29.
62. Tendulkar, *Mahatma*, vol. 2, 64.
63. 'We must know the meaning that the wearing of Khadi carries with it. Every time that we (wear it) [...] we should remember that we are doing so in the name of Daridranarayan and for the sake of the starving millions of India. If we have the "Khadi spirit" in us, we would surround ourselves with simplicity in every walk of life. The "Khadi spirit" means illimitable patience [...]. [Just as spinners have patience] even so must we have patience whilst we are spinning "the thread of Swaraj". The "Khadi spirit" means also an equally illimitable faith [...]. [Just as the spinner has faith] that the yarn he spins by itself small enough, put in the aggregate, would be enough to clothe every human being in India, so must we have illimitable faith in truth and non-violence ultimately conquering every obstacle in our way. The "Khadi spirit" means fellow feeling with every human being on earth. It means a complete renunciation of everything that is likely to harm our fellow creatures [...]. It ought to have the *tapashcharya* of those who are behind it [...]. If those who have consecrated their lives to *Khadi* will not incessantly insist on purity of life, *Khadi* is bound to stink in the nostrils of our countrymen.' M.K. Gandhi, *Khadi: Why and How* ed. Bharatan Kumarappa (Ahmedabad: Navajivan Publishing House, 1955), 104. *Tapashcharya* means voluntary self-sacrifice.
64. Cf. *CWMG*, vol. 27, 334.
65. The western media used the word 'loin-cloth' to refer to Gandhi's dress, which was, in fact, a *dhoti* that covered his waist up to his knees. When speaking and writing about his dress in English, Gandhi continued to use the word 'loin-cloth'. In this work I retain the popular English term as one word without the hyphen.
66. S.R. Tikekar, *Epigrams from Gandhiji* (Ahmedabad: Navajivan Trust, 1974/1994), 123.
67. *Ibid.*
68. Gandhi, *Hind Swaraj*, 24–25. Around the time of writing *Hind Swaraj*, Gandhi was keenly following from South Africa the 'discontent and unrest' in India. Cf. *CWMG*, vol. 7, 6.

4

Goffman: Gandhi as Performance Manager of a Nation

Honest, sincere, serious performance is less firmly connected with the solid world than one might first assume.... Ordinary social intercourse is itself put together as a scene is put together, by the exchange of dramatically inflated actions, counteractions, and terminating replies. Scripts even in the hands of unpracticed players can come to life because life itself is a dramatically enacted thing. All the world is not, of course, a stage, but the crucial ways in which it isn't are not easy to specify.[1]

Erving Goffman

In this chapter I explore Gandhi's ability to mould a public image of himself through his interaction with people. I will examine the performative element in his decision to dress in a loincloth. My theoretical framework will be the ethnography of the self of Erving Goffman (1922–1982) as elaborated in his seminal work, *The Presentation of Self in Everyday Life*. Goffman is considered by communication and sociology scholars to be among the most influential representatives of symbolic interaction theory.[2] He is respected for having brought a fresh dimension to the study of human social behaviour.[3] His greatest contribution to the communication sciences is the dramaturgical analysis of social relationships. The key to understanding Goffman is to observe incongruity in social behaviour closely.[4] Therefore, in observing Gandhi through Goffman's lens I am putting the authenticity of the Mahatma to the severest test.

Interaction and Credibility

When we enter the physical presence of others, there are many ways our audience can get to know us. If we are unacquainted, it combines the use of previous experience and any of the following ways to arrive at an inference of who we are: conduct, appearance, stereotypes, social setting, self-introduction or documentary self-identification. If already acquainted, the audience assumes that our characteristics which it knows from prior experience continue to persist. Besides these sources of information about us, however, the audience will also have to rely on the way we intentionally or unintentionally express ourselves through the occurrence of events in the course of the interaction.[5]

These expressions are of two types: *expressions we give* and *expressions we give off*. The former is the consciously expressed manner of communicating through language. The latter includes the wide range of nonverbal actions that may be either unintentional or intentional. Expressions given off, intentionally or not, say a lot about who we are, often much more than expressions we consciously give.[6]

Contrarily, social interaction not only reveals information but also conceals it because the crucial data that lie hidden within the interacting individuals are not always easy to read. For example, the access to our 'true' or 'real' attitudes, beliefs and emotions can be known only indirectly through the expressions that we give or we give off. Often, due to the many spatiotemporal constrains of everyday life, the veracity of these expressions are difficult to ascertain. Therefore, communication between interacting individuals has only a 'promissory' or inferential character. There are no statistical or scientific methods to determine an individual's credibility. In our self-presentation, our audience will have to accept us on faith.[7]

There is, however, a simple common sense way by which our audience will normally perform a credibility check on us. It will usually match the expressions we *give* against the expressions we *give off*. It will balance our verbal communication with our non-verbal communication. When there is no consistency between what we say and how we say it (or behave, appear, act, and so on), the result is *asymmetry*. When there is consistency between what we say and how we say it, there is *symmetry*.

However, the symmetry can be forced. When this happens, we use 'information games' that either intentionally or unintentionally manipulate the non-verbal aspects of our communication to match our verbal output before our audience. Goffman calls the information game 'a potentially infinite cycle of concealment, discovery, false revelation and rediscovery'.[8]

For instance, the smiles that one encounters at parties when making new acquaintances are usually etiquette strategies to appear polite. They may not really mean that people are truly delighted to make new acquaintances. It may be that they have attended the party against their will, solely to please an influential host, to show off their latest fashion or to enjoy a good meal.

Symmetry-manipulation occurs when we calculate our self-expression to obtain a specifically desired response; or when we control our ability to make a certain impression without being aware of the response it will invite; or when we consciously express ourselves in specific ways dictated by our status, culture or tradition. All these impression games are aimed at 'giving off' a set of impressions that usually accrue to our advantage as self-presenters before an audience.[9]

Goffman reminds us, however, that symmetry-manipulation cannot take the manipulator very far. For even when explicit self-projection has stopped the implicit self-projection of the non-verbal kind continues. 'Performers can stop giving expressions but cannot stop giving them off.'[10] In daily social interaction it is always the non-verbal signs that speak louder than words.

Gandhi and Symmetry

In applying Goffman's analysis of social interaction to Gandhi's behaviour in public places, one notes the constant striving for symmetry between what he believed and how he behaved. His passion for truthfulness—to himself, to society and to God—is the avowed purpose of writing his autobiography, unassumingly entitled, *The Story of My Experiments with Truth*.[11] Page after page speaks of his 'obsession' for symmetry—between words and deeds, between verbal and non-verbal communication, between the outer and inner selves, between political action and the spiritual quest:

> For me, truth is the sovereign principle, which includes numerous other principles. This truth is not only truthfulness in word, but truthfulness in thought also, and not only the relative truth of our conception, but

the Absolute Truth, the Eternal Principle, that is God [...]. Often in my progress I have had faint glimpses of the Absolute Truth, God, and daily the conviction is growing upon me that He alone is real and all else is unreal.[12]

Gandhi even warns his readers not to regard his writings as authoritative but only illustrative. They are useful only in as much as the reader, who is encouraged to carry on his own experiments in truth, wishes to benefit from them.[13] Contrary to Goffman's descriptions of the human tendency to indulge in impression games when presenting oneself in public, Gandhi declares that his exercise in sharing his experiments aims to make him child-like and 'humbler than the dust'.[14]

These attitudes of humility and discipleship at the feet of truth were not limited to words alone, they also affected how Gandhi dressed, how he presented himself non-verbally before the innumerable audiences he encountered, from the poorest to the richest, from the weakest to the most powerful. His desire to bring his exterior self in line with his interior principles was far from easy. It took him nearly 33 years.[15]

The spectrum of transformations began with the frivolous choices of youth. As a student of law in England (1888–1891) he was unwilling to compromise his traditional vegetarianism, but was eager to make up for the lack of sociability it caused by bringing his outward appearance in line with the best in British standards of civility.

During his early years in South Africa (1901–1906) he struggled with questions about Indian identity and imperial allegiance. He combined the English dress with the Indian turban. He was acutely conscious of preserving his status as a barrister by travelling first class and imposing a British culture on his family. Meanwhile he was drawn into fighting for justice and contesting the Empire's discriminatory laws against its Indian subjects.

Between 1906 and 1914, his experience in the Ambulance corps, the *brahmacharya* vow, Ruskin's *Unto this Last*, the experience of community living and his intense involvement in the struggle for indentured Indians gradually matured his commitment to personal integrity. His sartorial thinking may be summed up as follows: By wearing English-made cloth and dressing in English fashion, one expressed belief in English values and objectives; if one disagreed with such values one had no right to continue using the veneer of Englishness as one's second skin;

one's exterior performance had to match one's interior vision of reality or not at all.

To break from an English manner of dressing, however, meant finding a viable Indianised alternative to civility. He created a temporary substitute in 1906 through the *satyagraha* attire. It was a type of generalised 'clothing of subversion'. It revealed his awareness of the semiotic potentialities of cloth and clothing for a just cause. He deemed it a landmark in his quest for sartorial significance and had himself photographed in it. It was dignified and expressed the values he cherished: asceticism, simplicity and solidarity with the Indian masses in South Africa. His symmetry in word and behaviour was now more mature and advanced.

On returning to India in 1915, Gandhi permanently disassociated himself from an English sartorial identity. He disembarked on Indian soil in his Kathiawadi dress. It gave him the specificity that the *satyagraha* attire lacked. It was a highly localised dress, limited to his native Kathiawad region. It cheered the people of his home town who thronged to meet him. For Gandhi, it was a double home-coming—a return to his true culture and a new definition of civility.[16] Yet, its strength was also its greatest disadvantage. Its regional relevance implied that it did not speak to the wide variety of Indian cultures.

In 1917 he started out on his new quest for a pan-Indian alternative, one that would symbolise his inclusive aspirations for an India that was one, despite her differences in caste, culture, class and creed. He began to explore the possibility of an attire that no one community could appropriate as its own. This led him to experiment with various syntagmatic options: the *khadi*-woven *kurta-pyjama* or *kurta-dhoti*, worn with or without a turban and sometimes with or without a Gandhi *topi*. These models of attire were drawn from the masses and Gandhi was easily accepted by all groups without difficulty. They became the uniform of Indian nationalists who freely chose the combinations that suited their tastes.

However, such pan-Indian costumes did not sufficiently reflect the poverty of the majority of the population with whom the now revered 'Mahatma' wished to identify. Many of the poor in distant villages had far less on their frail bodies than the sartorial combinations suitable to nationalists. Gandhi's concern for those at the periphery aroused in him the determination to take one of his boldest steps: he would make his own body the medium through which he would invite the solidarity of the poor in the struggle for *swaraj*. This final transformation took place in 1921 when he divested himself of every inch of clothing as far as decency permitted and brought himself closer to the masses that were central to his concern. The sartorial quest had reached its zenith. Gandhi's clothing extolled simplicity, projected the essence of Indian civility, represented the poorest of the poor and defined his own identity and mission before the world.[17]

The symmetry between expressions given and given off, between his interior and exterior selves was now perfect. In his loin-clothed body Gandhi had found the spiritual stability and the psychological equilibrium to sustain his innumerable performances in the socio-political arena for the next 26 years of his very active life.

Defining a Social Situation

Goffman's thesis of symmetry and asymmetry in social interaction is not merely about the credibility of an individual before an acquainted or unacquainted audience. It is pre-eminently about defining a social situation. Just as we establish ways of being and relating through our symmetrical or asymmetrical behaviour in any social context, our witnesses, by virtue of their response to our self-presentation and to any lines of action we initiate, will also establish the type of social situation they prefer through their own symmetrical or asymmetrical behaviour.

The response of witnesses may be consensual or may conflict. Goffman's focus is on the former, where the participants tentatively agree to put aside their divergent feelings and ideas so that open contradictions may not occur. They decide through a surface agreement as to 'whose claims concerning what issues will be temporarily honoured.'[18] He calls this a *working consensus*.[19] It differs from situation to situation.

In accepting others' definitions of social situations, the initial information that people possess concerning fellow participants is crucial. All subsequent actions and responses would be orientated or slanted by these initial perceptions. They hold the key to the direction that planning and co-operation will take.

Gandhi's self-presentation on entering South Africa for the very first time is an appropriate example of the working consensus. As an England-educated barrister-at-law he was well dressed when he 'landed at Durban with a due sense of my importance.'[20] He was surprised to discover the snobbishness in the way the English treated him. Even Abdulla Sheth, the rich Indian client who had hired his services was startled on seeing him:

> Those who looked at me did so with a certain amount of curiosity. My dress marked me out from other Indians. I had a frock-coat and a turban, an imitation of the Bengal *pugree*. I was taken to the firm's quarters and shown into the room set apart for me, next to Abdulla Sheth's. He did not understand me. I could not understand him. He read the papers his brother had sent through me, and felt more puzzled. He thought his brother had sent him a white elephant. *My style of dress and living struck him as being expensive like that of the Europeans.*[21]

Gandhi was inadvertently defining the working consensus with his client through the wealthy first impression he was making by his attire. Goffman reiterates:

> [A]n individual can more easily make a choice as to what line of treatment to demand from and extend to the others present at the beginning of an encounter than he can alter the line of treatment that is being pursued once the interaction is underway [...]. First impressions are important.[22]

First impressions form definitions that gradually take on a moral character. They tell participants in social contexts how they *should* behave and what *ought* to be done in different encounters that follow. When persons violate these definitions and do not act in accordance with these moral promptings, social interaction is likely to suffer a breakdown. At stake in all social interaction is the moral credibility of individuals in the presence of others, which is tested on the basis of their self-projection, their definition of the social situation in which they present themselves and their ability to live in consistent symmetry with their projection and their definition.[23]

Gandhi was confronted with a similar dilemma when attending the Durban court for the first time in his frock coat and turban. He was asked by the Magistrate to take off his turban. He refused to do so and left the court. The papers reported the incident in an article entitled *An Unwelcome Visitor*. In an article written the same day, Gandhi tried to explain that the disobedience was not meant as an affront to the Magistrate. He was merely following an Indian custom in which one keeps one's head covered as a mark of respect to the authority present.

Since he would have to continue frequenting the courts as a professional lawyer, he thought of substituting his turban with a regular English hat. On discussing the idea with Abdulla Sheth, he was surprised to learn that with a hat he would be mistaken for a waiter and not a lawyer because in South Africa only Indians who were waiters wore English hats. Gandhi was in a quandary. Should he retain the turban and court controversy? Should he remove it and compromise his Indianness or switch to the English hat only to forego his professional identity? He decided to keep the turban. In doing so he defined for himself and his acquaintances who he was and how he wished to be treated:

> Society is organized on the principle that an individual who possesses certain social characteristics has a moral right to expect that others will value and treat him in an appropriate way. Connected with this principle is a second, namely that an individual who implicitly or explicitly signifies that he has certain social characteristics ought in fact to be what he claims he is. In consequence, when an individual projects a definition of the situation and thereby makes an implicit or explicit claim to be a person of a particular kind, he automatically exerts a moral demand upon the others, obliging them to value and treat him in the manner that persons of his kind have a right to expect. He also implicitly forgoes all claims to be things he does not appear to be and hence forgoes the treatment that would be appropriate for such individuals. The others find, then, that the individual has informed them as to what is and as to what they ought to see as the 'is'.[24]

Performances—Sincere and Cynical, Real and Contrived

Goffman defines a performance as 'all the activity of a given participant on a given occasion which serves to influence in any way any of the other participants.'[25] The participant who presents himself to others implicitly expects them to take him seriously, that is:

> [...] to believe that the character they see actually possesses the attributes he appears to possess, that the task he performs will have the consequences that are implicitly claimed for it, and that, in general, matters are what they appear to be.[26]

There is, however, a differing degree as to how much the expression presented as a social performance actually represents the true reality (Figure 4.1). At one extreme, a performer sincerely feels that whatever he is doing represents the true reality. He is 'taken in by his own act,' that is, 'he is sincerely convinced that the impression of reality which he stages is the real reality'.[27] Goffman calls this performance 'sincere'.

Figure 4.1: Audience Perception of Congruence in Performance

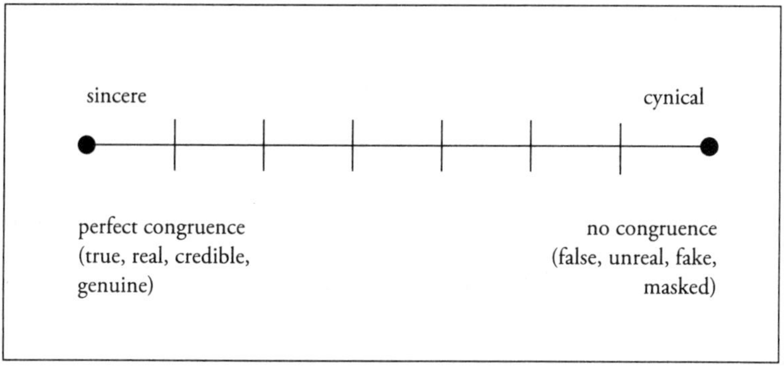

Source: Author.

At the other extreme, the performer is not taken in by his own act. He has no belief at all that his action stands for anything real. He is, as we commonly say, 'putting on an act'. This performance may be motivated by other ends that are not his own, and he may have no concern as to what impression he or his situation leaves on his audience. A good example of this is a government employee offering the clients a government service through a series of routines independent of his own likes or dislikes. Goffman calls this type of performance 'cynical'.[28]

Between the sincere and the cynical types of performance there are the different degrees of performance according to the sensitivity of the performer to the truth of his own actions, and to the awareness of his audience in accepting his performance as real or unreal, true or false, credible or fake, genuine or masked.

Most performances in everyday life—except stage-acting— are performed for an audience with the hope that they are received and accepted as real. In order to maintain this credibility, performers consciously or unconsciously resort to various tactics that help to control their glitches and slips, or, at least, prevent their audiences from noticing them. The more the incongruence, the greater is the effort to use sophisticated concealing mechanisms in order to present a credible appearance.

In Figure 4.2 two performances are indicated—one in which appearance is closer to reality and therefore does not need much impression management, the second in which appearance is propped up by impression tactics in order to hide audiences from discovering its remoteness from objective truth.

Goffman reminds us that in social interaction the real always appears, even if this appearance is minimal. However, the relation between appearance and reality is not intrinsic but statistical.[29] For example, honesty has to be performed to be credible because honesty does not exist in the abstract, locked up in a private mind, but in people who by nature engage in social interaction. Honesty has to reveal itself through credible

Figure 4.2: Management of Performance Credibility

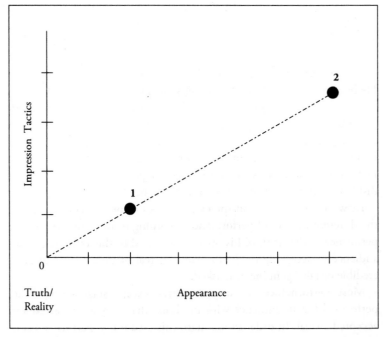

Source: Author.

social behaviour. Truth or reality by itself is a point, an invisible zero that does not exist until it makes its *social appearance* in some form. The sincerity owned has to be shown, and vice versa.

But here lies the rub. Since, according to Goffman, the relation between reality and appearance is statistical and not intrinsic, the degree of appearance with regard to the degree of honesty is adjustable: the really honest individual can choose to appear credible, just as a really dishonest person can manufacture a credible appearance. The greater the emphasis on appearance over reality, the more the need for tactics of impression management.[30]

This fundamental point in Goffman's performance theory, that is, the relation of appearance to reality in affecting interaction outcomes, is aptly demonstrated by Gandhi's own thinking. In the introduction to his *Autobiography*—a work he freely and willingly created so that his truth could make its first appearance before the world—he tells the readers to judge for themselves whether he is out to make an impression or whether he is sincere:

> If anything that I write in these pages should strike the reader as being touched with pride, then he must take it that there is something wrong with my quest, and that my glimpses are not more than mirage. Let hundreds like me perish, but let truth prevail [...]. I am not going either to conceal or understate any ugly things that must be told. I hope to acquaint the reader fully with all my faults and errors. My purpose is to describe experiments in the science of Satyagraha, not to say how good I am. In judging myself I shall try to be as harsh as truth, as I want others also to be.[31]

Tactics of Impression Management: 'Front'

'Front' is, as the word says, the foremost, visible and apparent part of an actor's performance. It is 'the expressive equipment of a standard kind intentionally or unwittingly employed by the individual during his performance.'[32] The front stands for standardised expressions or generalised representations that common people use to define situations in a general and fixed way. Goffman identifies two of these standard expressive equipments: setting and personal front.

Setting consists of the scenic, physical parts of the expressive equipment, associated with certain spatial location. Just as furniture, décor and physical design supply the stage props within which the actors perform, so also in everyday life, setting provides the fixed geography that surrounds the actor and gives meaning to his actions. The scenic elements add much to supplement the expression and communication in the actor's performance.[33]

Personal front is another item of expressive equipment 'that we most intimately identify with the performer himself and that we naturally expect will follow the performer wherever he goes'.[34] These include size, looks, colour, race, sex, age, body language, speech patterns, clothing, rank, and so on. While most of these signs are relatively fixed, some, like clothing or facial expressions, can vary within a performance or from one setting to the next. Accordingly, Goffman thinks it convenient to divide the characteristics of personal front into appearance and manner.

Appearance consists of those aspects that demonstrate social status. *Manner* signals the type of interaction performers expect to play in a given situation. For instance, haughtiness may indicate a show of dominance, while meekness may reveal a readiness to listen or be led.[35]

When individuals make their self-presentation in everyday situations, their audience assumes they are coherent. It expects to see a consistency between appearance and manner—that the social status they claim conforms to the performance they control. It expects that appearance and manner are also consistent with setting—that the social status and performance one expects is within the appropriate ambient that would warrant the respect it deserves. For example, a football coach expects discipline during training sessions on the football pitch and so do members of the team. At home on the other hand, the 'discipline' he would have to demand would not only differ qualitatively, but would also be perceived and recognised by members of his family in function of his roles as husband to his wife and father to his children. When there is perfect coherence we have the display of an ideal type personal front, one that fulfils the expected harmony of appearance, manner and setting. Lack of coherence in these elements that make up one's personal front are exceptions that become the stuff of news and gossip.

It is important to note that Goffman's understanding of coherence in the personal front is not to be confused with symmetry between expressions given and given off through one's behaviour. Nor is it the same as congruence between appearance and reality in one's perform-ance. The concept of front is a *tactic* of performance to conceal in-congruence and asymmetry. It feeds on standardised definitions (like stereotypes) of how one should appear, in what manner and in what setting. It does not deal with the deeper issues of the authenticity of a performer who may even ignore tactics or minimise their use in the quest for a more spontaneous self-expression.

When we look at Gandhi from a Goffman perspective we are once again confronted with a certain uniqueness that sets him apart from most world leaders—as is also proved by research studies on Gandhi's rhetorical charisma.[36] His choices as a front-man were a-typical and un-standardised in contrast with generally accepted behaviour under colonial rule. The settings in which he chose to act out his performances were often the lowliest places—the secluded Sabarmati *ashram*, the third class compartments, the out-caste *Bhanghi* colonies of Delhi, the shabbiest district in London, the nondescript Dandi shoreline and the inferno of hate called Noakhali. These settings were precisely where the marginal-ised of society battled for survival and recognition. His presence in their midst was neither an act of condescension nor a mere show of solidarity. He was earnest about placing them on the centre stage of the world, to be seen, heard and recognised. And because real poverty issues rarely provoked standard theatrical applause, Gandhi, conscious of his own popularity, ensured that the setting moved wherever *he* went and that he went where the *issues* mattered most. Goffman accommodates such a dramaturgical divergence from the stereotypical settings of everyday life as an exception relegated to very special cases:

> It is only in exceptional circumstances that the setting follows along with the performers; we see this in the funeral cortege, the civic parade, and the dream like processions that kings and queens are made of. In the main, these exceptions seem to offer some kind of extra protection for performers who are, or who have momentarily become, highly sacred. These worthies are to be distinguished, of course from quite profane performers of the peddler class who move their place of work between performances, often being forced to do so. In the matter of having one fixed place for one's setting, a ruler may be too sacred, a peddler too profane.[37]

Gandhi defined the social situation even in the presence of the powerful. In their company, that is, in the presence of dignitaries who enjoyed extremely sophisticated levels of front-maintenance and protocol, Gandhi's loin-clothed body was something of an embarrassment if not a cause for guilt. In western society, the coherence of appearance, manner and setting as a tactic of personal front is raised to the level of an art. There is a cultivated dignity in the way powerful personalities conduct themselves amidst highly staged environments and sophisticated protocol. Every spectacular detail is planned and every move rehearsed. Amidst such orchestrated ostentation, one can well imagine the prophetic persuasiveness of Gandhi's semi-nakedness that symbolised his people's cry for freedom. Whether conceded an audience with King George V[38] or refused one by Pope Pius XI;[39] whether welcomed by 'Il Duce' Mussolini[40] or shunned by Prime Minister Churchill,[41] it was this anti-symbol of power in a frail, diminutive body that conveyed a disturbing message[42]—a reminder to the Empires of Europe that their grand display of power could well be but an extravagant exercise in self-deception;[43] a reminder that the imperial show could go on no longer, not at the expense of millions among the coloured races of the world who were rendered naked, starving and enslaved.

Tactics of Impression Management: 'Dramatic Realisation', 'Idealisation', 'Mystification'

Human actions in the presence of others are fundamentally social in character and scope. As noted earlier, any social interaction involves a sharing of information that helps to define the situation in which people find themselves. However, not all information that is considered important by the participants is easily obtainable in casual conversation. A tactic that Goffman calls *dramatic realisation* is therefore necessary. 'While in the presence of others, the individual typically infuses his activity with signs which dramatically highlight and portray confirmatory facts that might otherwise remain unapparent or obscure.'[44] This explicitation of credentials can occur in split seconds and may be either voiced aloud or subtly demonstrated through the show of one's capabilities.

Some professions lend themselves to such dramatisation, such as can be seen in politicians, priests, educators, musicians, policemen and surgeons. Other professions have difficulty dramatising their capabilities. This often leads to the dilemma of whether professionals should focus on doing whatever they are doing 'for their own sake', or whether they should be concerned more about expressing what they are doing to others.

Non-governmental organisations engaged in social work are a case in point. A social worker engaged in the difficult task of caring for those at the periphery of society is obliged, at the same time, to demonstrate her credentials and her credibility before far off funding agencies situated in cities or wealthier countries. The only way she would be able to resolve this dilemma is to work together with others who form part of her organisation, but dedicate their time and energies to contacting and informing sponsors.

Here, Goffman's dramaturgical concept of 'front stage' and 'backstage' is highly relevant.[45] In any organisation, the real actors at the front stage who are in direct interaction with their audience are propped up by those at the backstage. In our example, the backstage administrative team supports the front stage social worker by producing glossy brochures and informative websites, by advertising on radio or television or by arranging extravagant concerts in aid of the poor beneficiaries. This dramatic realisation is undertaken with a view to ensuring that the social worker's credibility before the funding audience is promoted impressionably enough to fuel the organisation's administration costs and charities.

Goffman further notes that dramatic realisation by performers is created to impress, and is therefore construed with care. Whether intrinsic to the performer's role or elaborated by his/her backstage team, the information dramatically presented tends to be purified of errors before it is delivered to the target audience. Goffman calls this tactic *idealisation*. The idealised treatment of information is an attempt to hide the secret discrepancies between appearance and overall reality. Goffman lists five such secrets: profitable forms of activity connected with the performance;[46] the impression of infallibility by the correction or concealment of errors before the performance;[47] the demonstration of the product in its finished, polished and packaged state while hiding from public view the processes of its creation;[48] the concealment of all 'dirty work'—unclean, illegal, cruel, degrading;[49] the exhibition of the ideal motives, qualifications and challenges faced to acquire the role that reconstitutes the performer and sets him/her apart from lesser humans.[50]

To the extent that a performance demonstrates the official ideals and values of the society in which it occurs it becomes a ceremony—'an expressive rejuvenation and reaffirmation of the moral values of the community'.[51] To the extent also that this ceremonial display is believed in as real it has characteristics of a *celebration*. To stay away from it is to stay away from where reality is being performed. 'The world in truth is a wedding.'[52]

Idealisation tends to lead to another tactic called *mystification*. The rationale behind this higher level of impression management is as follows:

> If we see perception as a form of contact and communion, then control over what is perceived is control over contact that is made, and the limitation and regulation of what is shown is a limitation and regulation of contact. There is a relation here between informational terms and ritual ones. Failure to regulate the information acquired by the audience involves possible disruption of the projected definition of the situation; failure to regulate contact involves possible ritual contamination of the performer.[53]

Mystification is therefore a technique that may be employed to keep the observers in a sense of awe. The withholding of information is ritualised in such a way that distance is considered sacred and minimum contact with the performer becomes a blessing. Thus, observers are held in a state of mystified reverence for the performer. Maintenance of social distance and regulation of contacts are crucial if mystification as a tactic of managing impressions is to succeed.[54]

Gandhi, though shy at the start, turned out to be a 'genuine communicator'. His shyness taught him to measure the quality and method of his communication.[55] Motivated by his search for truth he let his communication emerge from the depths of his soul. He was not blind to the importance of demonstrating through words, gestures and symbols what he wished to say to his audiences. His presentation of self in public places was both strategic and authentic. His dress, for instance, was the result of a process of profound discernment on how his exterior self should best reflect his inner values and beliefs. His clothing was a symbol of his interior genuineness. It was not an impressionable tactic. He gradually learned that one's attire had another value, perhaps more important than simply representing one's beliefs: clothing could be used as a public statement on behalf of those who did not have enough to clothe themselves. Moreover, in a socially charged environment clothing also had the advantage of escaping political censorship. While the British government was adept at banning the newspapers it considered seditious, it was unaccustomed to censoring a clothing that was subversive. Gandhi's sartorial revolution amply demonstrated that seditious clothing could have a far greater impact on public opinion than seditious words. Thanks to the international publicity through photographs and reports, the thousands of *satyagrahis* who suffered violence at the hands of the British in *khadi* attire and Gandhi *topis* provided exceptionally dramatic effect to India's demand for freedom on the stage of the world. Gandhi was certainly aware of glitches and mistakes. The ulterior motives behind some of those who followed him pained him deeply. But he was realistic enough to see that erroneous cases were inevitable in the colossal task of converting millions to his truth.

Gandhi's personal clothing, notwithstanding its symbolic manifestation of an inner quest for authenticity, may still be appropriately perceived as Goffman's dramatised realisations. Accustomed to perceiving asceticism as the spiritual path of the sages and saints, the predominantly Hindu masses of India mystified, even deified Gandhi.[56] The title 'Mahatma', which Rabindranath Tagore is said to have conferred on him,[57] set him up as the spiritual leader of his people, notwithstanding Gandhi's disclaimer:[58]

> My experiments in the political field are now known, not only to India, but to a certain extent to the civilized world. For me, they have not much value; and the title of 'Mahatma' that they have won for me has, therefore, even less. Often the title has deeply pained me; and there is not a moment I can recall when it may be said to have tickled me.[59]

Yet, beyond the title itself, Gandhi's very lifestyle contributed to the mystification of 'the Leader with the halo'.[60] Combined with his voluntary poverty, simplicity, humility and *brahmacharya*, his frail body wrapped in a white loincloth communicated to the masses a rare spiritual force. For some, seeing him was the near equivalence of a pilgrimage to holy Banaras:[61]

> Curious crowds around Gandhi began to assume the form of throngs of devotees. Villagers travelled miles to have a Darshan—ceremonial glimpse of Gandhi. Mothers brought their ailing babies to be touched by Gandhi and to be healed. Long quests of peasants waited for a chance to

take the dust from his feet [...]. And for the time being, the hamlet where Gandhi pitched his tent became the hub of the nation.[62]

In the West too, a similar process of mystification was in motion.[63] To those who had read about him and followed keenly the part he was playing in imperial politics, the mere utterance of his name conjured up images of Christ on the Cross.[64]

For Gandhi, however, the adoption of the austere manner of dressing had nothing to do with a desire to manifest saintliness, nor to attract *darshan*.[65] He attached no religious significance to the loincloth. It was only a reminder to Indians to start spinning and weaving so that the poor could be decently clothed.[66] Nonetheless, the total complexity of his rich personality spoke for itself. He needed no back-stage props for a well-orchestrated propaganda. He was the front stage and he was totally in control of the agenda he set for himself and the future of India. Even at the dawn of Independence when Congress was preparing to be the government of the new-born nation in Delhi the centre of power, Gandhi was walking barefooted on the thorny mud paths of riot-stricken villages of Noakhali as a 'one man boundary force' against violence and communal hatred. He brought the senseless massacre to a halt on the strength of his fast unto death. The cameras followed him but he followed no camera. The construction of his own performances was not motivated by egotism but by the demands of truth and the urgency for peace.

Staging and the Self

The presentation of the self before others is a necessary part of every social interaction. Goffman goes a step further. In every social interaction the structure of the self is necessarily disclosed. The individual who presents self can be, for reasons of analysis, divided into *performer*, the agent involved in staging a performance, and *character*, the figure or model that the performance was designed to evoke. These two sets have different attributes but both have significance only in the staged performance, that is, 'in terms of the show that must go on'.[67]

The *character that is performed* in contemporary society is often equated with the self, almost as if the self (the cause) resides within the character (the effect). But Goffman considers this unidirectional analysis inadequate. His work shows that the character is not derived from the self as a possessor but 'from the whole scene of his action, being generated by that attribute of local events which renders them interpretable by witnesses'.[68] The self is a product of a staged sequence, not the cause of it:

> The self [...] as a performed character, is not an organic thing that has a specific location, whose fundamental fate is to be born, to mature, and to die; it is a dramatic effect arising diffusely from a scene that is presented, and the characteristic issue, the crucial concern, is whether it will be credited or discredited.[69]

In analysing the self in performance theory, we are not merely concerned about the self as possessor—the embodied person behind the character (which Goffman calls 'the peg on which the collaborative manufacture will be hung for a time'.[70]) We are concerned about the self as a character performed. We are dealing with a complex performance framework within which the embodied performing self is projected as a character (Figure 4.3). This construction involves backstage tools for body shaping and adornment, front stage structures having fixed props, a team of persons that will create and present the scene to fit the character, and finally, the audience that will interpret and respond in ways

Figure 4.3: The Performing Self in a Social Situation

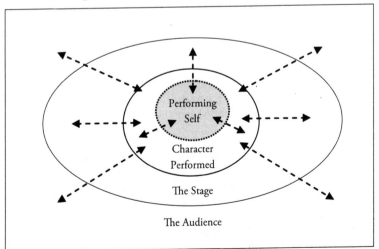

Source: Author.

that make the character emerge.[71] The self as character is a product of these arrangements. Seen in this perspective 'the whole machinery of self-production is cumbersome'.[72] It runs the risk of a breakdown. And when it does, either it yields to embarrassing exposure, or a smooth impression management plan is quickly put in place to give the appearance that the character emanates intrinsically from the performer.[73]

The *performing self* is the organic, embodied subject whose fate is to be born, to mature and to die. It has the capacity to learn and to train for a part in the many social interactions of everyday life. It has dreams of successful performances and nightmares of embarrassing failures. It takes pleasure in encouragement and dreads reproach in public. Due to its sense of shame it attempts to minimise exposure to situations that would bring discredit.[74] These attributes of the individual *qua* performer are not merely a depicted effect of particular performances; they are psychobiological in nature, and yet they seem to arise out of intimate interaction with the contingencies of staging performances.[75]

In the light of Goffman's theory, two passages from Gandhi's writings will reveal the tension he experienced between his inner self and the character he wished to portray in two separate social interactions. In the first example as a student in England around 1889, he describes the compromises his friendship with an Englishman demanded. He is at pains to let his performing self adjust to the cultural demands of loyalty through the creation of a character that, according to him, would help safeguard the relationship:

> My (non-vegetarian) friend had not ceased to worry about me. His love for me led him to think that, if I persisted in my objections to meat eating, I should not only develop a weak constitution, but should remain a duffer, because I should never feel at home in English society [...].

> But I decided that I should put him at ease, that I should assure him that I would be clumsy no more, but try to become polished and make up for my vegetarianism by cultivating other accomplishments which fitted one for polite society. And for this purpose I undertook the all too impossible task of becoming an English gentleman.

> The clothes after the Bombay cut that I was wearing were, I thought, unsuitable for English society, and I got new ones at the Army and Navy Stores. I also went in for a chimney-pot hat costing nineteen

shillings—an excessive price in those days. Not content with this, I wasted ten pounds on an evening suit made in Bond Street, the centre of fashionable life in London; and got my good and noble-hearted brother to send me a double watch chain of gold. It was not correct to wear a ready-made tie and I learnt the art of tying one for myself. While in India, the mirror had been a luxury permitted on the days when the family barber gave me a shave. Here I wasted ten minutes every day before a huge mirror, watching myself arranging my tie and parting my hair in the correct fashion […].

As if this were not enough to make me look the thing I directed my attention to other details that were supposed to go towards the making of an English gentleman […].[76]

Contrast this experience with Gandhi's last major change in attire. The example above demonstrates how the performing self bent double to project an acceptable *character*. The choice for the loincloth instead reveals how Gandhi's *performing self* was firmly in control despite the embarrassment to the character performed.

In his enthusiasm to increase the participation in the boycott of foreign cloth, Gandhi invited even the very poor to give up their foreign clothing and wear *khadi*. In Madurai, on learning that the poor could not afford *khadi* because it was costlier than British cloth, he challenged his emaciated audience to wear *khadi* loincloths instead. This harsh appeal from a well-clothed speaker to a helplessly impoverished people disturbed his conscience. He knew he lacked the courage to practise what he preached. He went through an ordeal of introspection in the effort to be honest to himself and the poor. He finally made his daring choice on 22 September 1921:

> I give the advice under a full sense of my responsibility. In order therefore to set the example I propose to discard at least up to the 31st of October [1921] my *topi* and vest and to content myself with only a loin-cloth and a *chaddar* whenever found necessary for the protection of the body. I adopt the change because I have always hesitated to advise anything I may not myself be prepared to follow, also because am anxious by leading the way to make it easy for those who cannot afford to change on discarding their foreign garments.[77]

All the alterations I have made in my course of life have been effected by momentous occasions; and they have been made after such a deep deliberation that I have hardly had to regret them. And I did them, as I could not help doing them.[78]

The passion for coherence between the performing self and the performed character was overwhelming. Yet, the performing self was not without doubts and the fear of human respect:

> The masses in Madras watch me [in a loincloth] with bewilderment [...]. But if India calls me a lunatic, what then? If the co-workers do not copy my example, what then? Of course this is not meant to be copied by co-workers. It is meant simply to hearten the people, and to make my way clear. Unless I went about with a loin-cloth, how might I advise others to do likewise? What should I do where millions have to go naked? At any rate why not try the experiment for a month and a quarter? Why not satisfy myself that I left not a stone unturned? [...] It is after all this thinking that I took this step. I (now) feel so very easy [...]. *I want the reader to measure from this the agony of my soul.*[79]

This sensitivity to coherence between performing self and performed character is unique to Gandhi's charismatic leadership. It is unparalleled in world political history. While most leaders improve their performances with a view to sustain the attention of their audiences, Gandhi sought 'to turn the searchlight inward'.[80] He strove to make his appearance truthful and his truthfulness apparent. The harmony between the inner and outer selves was a constant preoccupation at the base of his 'experiments with truth'.[81] 'As I searched myself deeper, the necessity for changes both internal and external began to grown on me.'[82] These changes 'harmonized my inward and outward life [...]. My life was certainly more truthful and my soul knew no bounds of joy.'[83]

Gandhi: Performance Manager of a Nation

Gandhi's approach to the presentation of himself in everyday life is a daringly different model in comparison to the vast number of examples cited by Goffman in his research. While most of these examples reveal how persons are generally motivated by self-esteem, group-think or social structures to project favourable characters, Gandhi's motives move him in the opposite direction. Not immune to the performative routines that were a natural part of his role as a politician, his heightened self-awareness and self-discipline constantly purified the integrity of his performances so that they emanated from his fidelity to truth. That this was performance at its most daring, no one can deny.

But the evidence also suggests that Gandhi's performances were strong stimulants for others to get into the act.[84] He drew crowds to disobey civilly, non-cooperate non-violently, march a near 240 mile dirt-track to the sea, defy imperial laws and court arrests. His fasts that were broadcast nationally and internationally brought violence to a halt on perilously critical occasions.[85] For 30 years he gave public discourses and prayed openly with his countrymen and women, persuading them to rally round a common agenda of *his choice.*

Gandhi was more than just a performer, he was the performance manager of an entire nation-in-waiting. That meant motivating nearly 300 million Indians to *satyagraha* against 100,000 English—a performance that was conceived, designed, scripted, promoted and staged by Gandhi alone. In December 1921, the Indian National Congress met to appoint him as its sole executive authority. He was the 'front' that called the shots—both before his audience as well as backstage, where the Congress learned to immerse itself in co-directing the greatest people's revolution the world has ever seen. In homes, public places, remote villages or important cities; through shop-picketing, street-marching, spinning homespun or boycotting foreign cloth—*khadi* gave the performances a powerful visual quality. The greatest Empire on earth was rendered helpless as *khadi* put subversion on parade.

Truly, performance was intrinsic to the Swadeshi Movement even in personal sacrifice. It was designed to attract arrests, just as Gandhi planned: 'Freedom is to be wooed only inside prison walls and sometimes on gallows.'[86] The ideal non-co-operator would have to seek imprisonment in order to convert the unjust Government. Arrests were to be sought 'not rudely, roughly, blushingly, certainly never violently, but peacefully, quietly, courteously, humbly, prayerfully, and courageously'.[87] In the span of just two months—December 1921 and January 1922—nearly 30,000 people were imprisoned.[88] When Gandhi himself was arrested in 1922, he accepted responsibility for the violent outbreaks which had mistakenly occurred, and which were never part of his plan. He asked for the highest penalty that could be inflicted on him. The sincerity and power of this attitude was so novel it even made the experienced Judge Broomfield admit that Gandhi was in a different category from any person that he had ever tried or was likely to try. He expressed his dilemma—so typical of Goffman's distinctions of the performing subject and the performed character—in these memorable words:

> The law is no respecter of persons. Nevertheless it would be impossible to ignore the fact that in the eyes of millions of your countrymen you are a great patriot and a great leader. Even those who differ from you in politics, look upon you as a man of high ideals and of noble and even saintly life. *I have to deal with you in one character only* [...]. It is my duty to judge you as a man subject to the law, who has, by his own admission, broken the law.[89]

Gandhi, as leader of a people's performance on the road to independence, had proved that dramaturgical personalities are not merely the result of social interaction. Great performers need deeper foundations to sustain the powerful interactive forces that can beat them down. Goffman calls this foundation 'dramaturgical discipline':

> A performer who is disciplined, dramaturgically speaking, is someone who remembers his part and does not commit unmeant gestures or faux pas in performing it. He is someone with discretion [...]. He is someone with 'presence of mind' [...]. And if disruption of the performance cannot be avoided or concealed, the disciplined performer will be prepared to offer a plausible reason for discounting the disruptive event, a joking manner to remove its importance, or deep apology and self-abasement to reinstate those held responsible for it. The disciplined performer is also someone with 'self-control'. He can suppress his emotional response to his private problems, to his team-mates when they make mistakes, and to the audience when they induce untoward affection or hostility in him [...]. And the disciplined performer is someone with sufficient poise to move from private places of informality to public ones of varying degrees of formality, without allowing such changes to confuse him.[90]

The influence Gandhi's disciplined performance had on a once voiceless and faceless people through the unique power of his charisma had no precedent. He became 'a symbolic expression of the confused desires of the people'.[91] Or in the words of his grandson, Rajmohan Gandhi, he was 'a metaphor and a standard'.[92]

Notes

1. Erving Goffman, *The Presentation of the Self in Everyday Life* (New York: Anchor Books, 1959), 71–72. (Henceforth *PSEL*).

2. 'Although Goffman is admired by everyone, it is also fair to say that many symbolic interactionists feel uncomfortable using his ideas. This is because both these sub-traditions arguably lead away from the study of lived human experience in the way this was understood by George Herbert Mead and Herbert Blumer.' Max Travers, *Qualitative Research through Case Studies* (London: Sage Publications 2001), 59.

3. Herbert Blumer who coined the term 'symbolic interactionism' criticised Goffman's work as impoverishing our understanding of human beings by limiting a study of them to one perspective alone—the fact that they perform for an audience, even when they are not consciously doing so. He thinks that Ethnography, which he (Blumer) advocates, attempts to present a much more rounded picture of human beings and their behaviour in any given setting of social interaction, which, in his reckoning, Goffman has not strictly adhered to. Cf. Travers, *Qualitative Research*, 60.

4. Cf. Rod Watson, 'Reading Goffman on Interaction,' in *Goffman and Social Organization: Studies in a Sociological Legacy*, ed. G. Smith (London: Routledge, 1999), 138–55. Kenneth Burke calls the technique used by Goffman 'a perspective by incongruity'. Cf. Travers, *Qualitative Research*, 51.

5. Cf. Goffman, *PSEL*, 1–2.

6. Cf. Goffman, *PSEL*, 2.

7. Cf. Goffman, *PSEL*, 2–3. Goffman elaborates by quoting William I. Thomas: 'It is also highly important for us to realise that we do not as a matter of fact lead our lives, make our decisions, and reach our goals in everyday life either statistically or scientifically. We live by inference. I am, let us say, your guest. You do not know, you cannot determine scientifically, that I will not steal your money or your spoons. But inferentially I will not, and inferentially you have me as a guest.'

8. Goffman, *PSEL*, 7–8.

9. Cf. Goffman, *PSEL*, 6.

10. Goffman, *PSEL*, 108.

11. The *Autobiography* is a compendium of memories of Gandhi's personal battle with the 'canker of untruth'. What is most significant is the transparency and coherence in the retelling. It is my opinion that the *Autobiography* alone is excellent material for a Goffmanian research on the presentation of self—a topic, perhaps, for another thesis.

12. Gandhi, *Autobiography*, xiii–xiv.

13. Cf. Gandhi, *Autobiography*, xiv.

14. *Ibid.*

15. I refer to the period of sartorial transformations from Gandhi's arrival in England as a student of law in 1888 to his decision to adopt the loincloth in 1921. See corresponding photographs on pages 129–31. For a detailed biographical study of his clothing

evolution see Peter Gonsalves, 'Half-naked Fakir'—The Story of Gandhi's Personal Search for Sartorial Integrity,' *Gandhi Marg*, 31 (1, April–June 2009): 5–30.

16. 'With my Kathiawadi cloak, turban and dhoti, I looked somewhat more civilized than I do today.' Gandhi, *Autobiography*, 344.

17. The original quotation reads: Gandhi said, he 'divest[ed] [him]self of every inch of clothing [he] decently could and thus to a still greater extent [brought himself] in line with the ill-clad masses […] in so far as the loin cloth also spells simplicity let it represent Indian civilization'. Jaju Shrikrishnadas, *The Ideology of Charka*, Tirupur: The A.I.S.A. Khaddar Malar and Sarvodaya Prachuralayam for The All India Spinners Association, Sevagram, 1951, p. 99, cited by Bean, *Cloth and Human Experience*, 367.

18. Goffman, *PSEL*, 9–10.

19. Cf. *ibid.*, 10.

20. M.K. Gandhi, *Satyagraha in South Africa*, (Ahmedabad: Navajivan Publishing House,1928) online version by Yann Forget, 2003, 33: http://www.forget-me.net/en/Gandhi/satyagraha.pdf (retrieved: 12 April 2007).

21. Gandhi, *Autobiography*, 98.

22. Goffman, *PSEL*, 11.

23. Cf. Goffman, *PSEL*, 12.

24. Goffman, *PSEL*, 13.

25. Goffman, *PSEL*, 15.

26. Goffman, *PSEL*, 17.

27. *Ibid.*

28. Goffman, *PSEL*, 18.

29. Goffman, *PSEL*, 71.

30. Cf. Goffman, *PSEL*, 70–76.

31. *Ibid.*

32. Goffman, *PSEL*, 22.

33. *Ibid.*

34. Goffman, *PSEL*, 24.

35. *Ibid.*

36. Cf. Bligh and Robinson, *Different Routes to Charisma*: www.cgu.edu/include/flm-spr04.pdf (24 May 2005).

37. Goffman, *PSEL*, 22.

38. The visit took place on 5 November 1931 at a reception in honour of the delegates of the Round Table Conference. Gandhi had a five minute talk with the King. Cf. W.L. Shirer, *Gandhi: A Memoir* (New York: Simon & Schuster, 1979), 166.

39. Gandhi visited the Vatican on 12 December 1931. The Pope did not receive him. Documents in the Vatican's Secret Archives do not explain the exact reason for this refusal. A passionate letter from an American Catholic to the Pope attests that newspapers in the USA cite the Vatican's strict adherence to a dress code as the motive. Cf. Segreteria di Stato, 1931, rubrica 351, protocollo 106979: 'Gandhi. Notizie circa sua venuta a Roma,' *Archivio Segreto Vaticano* (researched: 26–28 April 2007). Also see the *Universal* newsreel dated 13 December 1931 (Clip Id, fopemg1931125004_3105_4501) which is entitled, 'Gandhi's Scant

Garb bars Papal Audience,' http://www.gandhiserve.org/footage/fopemg_1931. html (1 December 2007).

40. Gandhi was invited by Benito Mussolini to the Palazzo Venezia on the morning of 12 December 1931. Witnesses describe the 10 minute meeting as 'a cordial, but politically insignificant chat and it was nearly always Mussolini who did the talking'. Cf. Gianni Sofri, 'Gandhi in Fascist Italy,' in *Gandhi and India*, ed. Sofri Gianni (Gloucestershire: The Windrush Press, 1999), 108. Mirabehn (Madeleine Slade), daughter of a British admiral and Gandhi's disciple accompanied Gandhi on his visit to Europe and recalled this meeting many years later: 'Mussolini turned to speak to Bapu (Gandhi) in excellent English and asked a number of questions regarding India [...]. When ten minutes were over, he rose from his chair, giving us the sign that the audience was over, and he accompanied us to the door at the end of the room. The General (Moris) [Gandhi's host in Rome] told us later that this behaviour was very unlike Mussolini's, who usually does not rise from his chair, and never raises his eyes when his visitors enter.' Translated from Gianni Sofri, *Gandhi in Italia* (details not cited), quoted in Di Luigi Capano, 'Gandhi in Italia per conoscere il Fascismo,' 14 January 2007, in *Italia Sociale* website: http://www. italiasociale.org/storia07/storia140107-1.html (5 September 2007).

41. Winston Churchill led the opposition to India's self-government. He denounced the meeting of the Viceroy of India, Lord Irwin, with Gandhi and refused to meet the latter when he visited England for the Second Round Table Conference. Speaking at the Constitutional Club on 26 March 1931, he observed that 'Gandhi, with deep knowledge of the Indian peoples, by the dress he wore—or did not wear, by the way in which his food was brought to him at the Viceregal Palace, deliberately insulted, in a manner which he knew everyone in India would appreciate, the majesty of the King's representative. These are not trifles in the East. Thereby our power to maintain peace and order among the immense masses of India has been sensibly impaired.' Ramachandra Guha, 'Churchill and Gandhi', *The Hindu*, 19 June 2005, online version:http://www.hindu.com/mag/2005/06/19/ stories/2005061900060300.htm (4 September 2007). Also see Rajmohan Gandhi, *The Good Boatman—A Portrait of Gandhi* (New Delhi: Penguin Books, 1997), 92, 111–12.

42. As an example of Gandhi's 'uncomfortable message' it is worth recalling Churchill's lamentation of the Gandhi–Irwin pact that brazenly reveals his cultural prejudices. He found it 'nauseating' and 'alarming' to think that the 'half-naked fakir' parleyed 'on equal terms with the representative of the King-emperor'. In his opinion, the pact was an appeasement extended to Indians in a manner that had 'inflicted such humiliation and defiance as has not been known since the British first trod the soil of India'. Cf. R. Gandhi, *The Good Boatman*, 112.

43. This is an allusion to the popular fairy tale of Hans Christian Andersen: 'The Emperor's New Clothes' (1837). Like the little child who innocently drew attention to the King's nakedness as he naively enjoyed the adulation of his people, Gandhi drew the attention of the empires to their moral blindness by symbolising through his semi-nakedness, the oppressive effects of imperial greed on the colonised races.

44. Goffman, *PSEL*, 30.

45. Cf. Goffman, *PSEL*, 106–40.
46. Cf. Goffman, *PSEL*, 43.
47. Cf. Goffman, *PSEL*, 43–44.
48. Cf. Goffman, *PSEL*, 44.
49. Cf. *ibid.*
50. Cf. Goffman, *PSEL*, 46–48.
51. Goffman, *PSEL*, 35.
52. Goffman, *PSEL*, 36.
53. Goffman, *PSEL*, 67.
54. Cf. Goffman, *PSEL*, 67–70.
55. 'My hesitancy in speech, which was once an annoyance, is now a pleasure. Its greatest benefit has been that it has taught me the economy of words. I have naturally formed the habit of restraining my thoughts. And I can now give myself the certificate that a thoughtless word hardly ever escapes my tongue or pen.' Gandhi, *Autobiography*, 58.
56. Most of the photographs in the 312-page compilation by Peter Rühe testify to the great reverence people had for Gandhi. Cf. Rühe, *Gandhi*.
57. Cf. Krishna Dutta and Andrew Robinson, *Rabindranath Tagore: An Anthology* (London: Macmillan, 1997), 2. Other sources state that Nautamlal Bhagavanji Mehta accorded him this title on 21 January 1915. Cf. *Kamdartree*: http://kamdartree.com/mahatma_kamdar.htm (4 March 2007).
58. Gandhi openly expressed his uneasiness at being treated with such reverence: 'I have disclaimed the title of a saint for I am fully conscious of my limitations and imperfections. I claim to be a servant of India and therethrough of humanity.' *CWMG*, vol. 26, 333.
59. Gandhi, *Autobiography*, xii. See his reaction to the protests against the alleged erection of his statue at the cost of Rs 25,000. Without awaiting confirmation he reinforces the protest of his correspondents by agreeing fully with them, hoping that, if it be a rumour, his lines will serve as a warning to those who wish to honour him in like manner. *CWMG*, vol. 68, 386.
60. Cf. Shridharani, *War without Violence*, 220–47.
61. Cf. Nanda, *Mahatma Gandhi*, 212.
62. Shridharani, *War without Violence*, 223–24.
63. See the 'mystifying' tributes paid to Gandhi in Sarvepalli Radhakrishnan, *Mahatma Gandhi: Essays and Reflections on his Life and Work* (Mumbai: Jaico Publishing House, 2004); in particular, the tributes of Lawrence Binyon (p. 52), Carl Heath (p. 82), John H. Holmes (p. 105), and Maude Petre (p. 222).
64. Cf. Bean, *Cloth and Human Experience*, 368.
65. On Gandhi's opinion of *darshan* see, *CWMG*, vol. 21, 326.
66. Cf. Markovits, *The Un-Gandhian Gandhi*, 31.
67. Cf. Goffman, *PSEL*, 252. Note the similarity in Saussure's and Barthes's use of signifier (performer), signified (character) the sign (the staged performance) and the sign system (the staged sequence).
68. *Ibid.*
69. Goffman, *PSEL*, 252–53.
70. Cf. Goffman, *PSEL*, 253.

71. Cf. *ibid.*
72. *Ibid.*
73. Cf. *ibid.*
74. Cf. *ibid.*
75. Goffman, *PSEL*, 254.
76. Gandhi, *Autobiography*, 47–48.
77. *CWMG*, vol. 21, 180.
78. *Ibid.*, p. 181.
79. *Ibid.*, p. 226 (emphasis mine). In a letter to his personal secretary, Mahadev Desai, on 23 September 1921 he wrote: 'You must have noticed the great change I have introduced in my dress—I could bear the pain no longer.'
80. *CWMG*, vol. 21, 122.
81. 'I devote my energy to the propagation of non-violence as the law of our life —individual, social, political, national and international. I fancy that I have seen the light, though dimly. I write cautiously, for I do not profess to know the whole of the Law. If I know the successes of my experiments, I know also my failures. But the successes are enough to fill me with undying hope.' *CWMG*, vol. 68, 390.
82. Gandhi, *Autobiography*, 51.
83. *Ibid.*
84. Nehru is an eloquent witness to the mood of volunteers who experienced the extraordinary nature of Gandhi's influence at the start of the Freedom Struggle: 'I became wholly absorbed and wrapt in the movement, and large numbers of other people did likewise. I gave up all my other associations and contacts, old friends, books, even newspapers, except in so far as they dealt with the work in hand. I had kept up till then some reading of current books and had tried to follow the developments of world affairs. But there was no time for this now. In spite of the strength of my family bonds, I almost forgot my family, my wife, my daughter […] I lived in offices and committee meetings and crowds. "Go to the villages" was the slogan, and we trudged many a mile across fields and visited distant villages and addressed peasant meetings. I experienced the thrill of mass-feeling, the power of influencing the mass.' Nehru, *An Autobiography*, 82–83.
85. The occasions were to restore peace after the visit of the Prince of Wales in November 1921, and to stop communal riots between Hindus and Muslims in September 1924 and September 1947.
86. Cited by Nanda, *Mahatma Gandhi*, 241.
87. *Ibid.*
88. Cf. *ibid.*
89. Nanda, *Mahatma Gandhi*, 40.
90. Goffman, *PSEL*, 216–17.
91. Nehru, *An Autobiography*, 81.
92. R. Gandhi, *The Good Boatman*, ix.

5

A Gandhian Approach to Symbolisation[1]

Khadi to me is the symbol of unity of Indian humanity, of its economic freedom and equality and, therefore, ultimately, in the poetic expression of Jawaharlal Nehru, 'the livery of India's freedom'.[2]

M.K. Gandhi

We human beings are symbol-makers by definition. We create symbols to express our individual identities and to emphasise the quality of our relationships. They are blessings we give each another. They help us share meanings beyond the limitation of our contexts. They create community and build common interests. They infuse us with the courage to change unjust regimes. They appeal to the best in us to serve the rest of us, especially those less fortunate than we are.

We humans are also symbol-abusers. We can create symbols to lie, to mislead, to hypnotise, to manipulate and to diminish the power of reason, volition and conscience. We can use symbols as fixed patterns for perceiving reality through assumptions, judgements, accusations and condemnations of the unfamiliar 'other'. In the hands of bigots and demagogues, symbols can be used to turn humanity against its very self.

Symbols are not isolated entities. They create and dwell within cultures—cultures of life or death, peace or war, tolerance or hatred, cooperation or competition, altruism or consumerism, discipline or anarchy. Symbols that create qualitatively new cultures have a transformative power to subvert the status quo. Symbols that are part of dominant cultures, however, hinder the formation of critical consciousness by normalising and naturalising interpretations and behaviours. They reinforce and maintain banal world views against those that are new or those that have prophetic potential to bring about constructive social change.

All in all, symbols are *made* in the image and likeness of their creators—which is why it is most important to know who creates the symbols we consume, who controls the symbol-making processes, what are the values symbol-makers live by and what are their ultimate goals. We need to look behind the symbols to the histories of the symbol-makers themselves, who, by reason of their competence, or social privileges wield the power to uplift or destroy humanity, or to fleece one part of humanity for the benefit of another.

In studying Gandhi as a symbol-maker, I have chosen to accentuate a benchmark in the history of symbolisation for socio-political change.[3] It is not merely the quantity of symbols he produced or the wide breadth of his communication skills that gives him pre-eminence as a leader and the subject of prodigious multidisciplinary research, but the quality and process of symbol-making as well. Gandhi's symbolisation of *swaraj*, *swadeshi*, *satyagraha* and *ahimsa* 'set and attained personal standards of conviction and courage that few will ever match. He was that rare kind of leader who was not confined by the inadequacies of his followers.'[4]

What was Gandhi's Communication Secret?

My historical research and communication analysis on Gandhi's clothing for liberation spur me on to identify six principles as constitutive of a Gandhian approach to symbolisation.

Historical analysis

Gandhian symbolisation is a radical process. It involves a patient study and rigorous analysis of the root causes behind the problematic issues in a given society. It does not superimpose symbols from extraneous contexts as quick-fix solutions but lets the context germinate its own seeds of new meaning. Only after being well informed about the past through objectively balanced scholarship[5] can the symbol-maker work out appropriate responses to present ills. The foundation of Gandhian symbol-making implies living with a sense of history in order to make sense of the 'here and now'.

Grass-root experience

Another indispensable part of the Gandhian process of symbolisation is the understanding of contexts from within and from below. This means immersing oneself fully in a situation so as to observe intelligently the dynamics for an appropriate symbolic response. Gandhian communicators are not library bookworms. They do not pontificate from a stable high-ground, hemmed in by the walls, securities and privileges of substantial emoluments. Nor do they imitate foreign models of civility. They seek new reference points that emerge from the strengths, perspectives, wisdom and experiences of the most disadvantaged sections of society. They position themselves where dusty feet, soiled hands, sweating bodies and broken hearts grapple with life's daily uncertainties. It is from experiences like these that they will create the symbols that touch common people and move the conscience of the world.

The scientific temper

Gandhian symbol-makers are indefatigable seekers of Truth, the *raison d'être* underlying their historical and experiential quest. Truth is also the final cause that lifts them beyond the dross and muddle of social entanglements. In the crosstalk of heated debate, they do not pit one opponent against the other, but attempt to understand and empathise with the arguments on both sides. They take pains to perceive the veracity of things, aware of the supreme importance of interpreting reality accurately in order to reconstruct it in their symbols. They cultivate a scientific approach to the assessment of issues-in-context by being wary of the subtle and often unconscious intrusions of their own prejudices and passions. They let their verbal or non-verbal symbolisation flow from their genuine striving for intellectual, emotional and spiritual honesty.[6]

Ethical religion

Responsibility is the watch-word of Gandhian communicators. The joy of living comes from a commitment to bring social reality in line with *dharmic* righteousness, the Divine Plan. This being the ultimate end, all the means employed to reach it must necessarily be coherent. It is not merely the goal that counts but also the way to get there. Gandhian symbol-makers acknowledge the need to focus their energies on the moral way by engaging in action and not merely in words. They act whenever justice and truth are violated, but always in the sprit of *nishkama-karma*: for the sake of duty itself, never for its fruits. The perfection of their action is its own reward. Such detachment may even demand their own death. Giving one's life for a cause is the supreme symbol. It is their best message to the world.

Oneness of reality

All symbolisation has value only insofar as it reflects the Truth, the One and Only Reality. All else is illusion, or deception masquerading as truth. 'An error does not become truth by reason of multiplied propagation, nor does truth become error because nobody sees it. Truth stands, even if there be no public support. It is self sustained.'[7] This foundational principle underpins the clarity of mind and heart, the resoluteness and the purpose that Gandhian symbol-makers require, steeped as they are in the ebb and flow of a thousand daily decisions. They know that beyond everything that obfuscates and divides, there is the One that unites all. The more they are able to interpret reality from this inclusive perspective, the easier it is to recognise the wastefulness of rancour, vendetta and violence. They see the value of their symbol-making-identity as a participation in the Reality that calls all beings to unity, that draws all persons and events to communion and peace.

Socio-political transformation

The Gandhian framework is by its very nature an undercurrent of non-violent subversion thrusting towards *purna swaraj*. It is subversive, not because human beings and the social structures they create are evil, but because true freedom always eludes our actual human constructions of it. 'Real liberation will come not by the acquisition of authority by a few, but by acquisition of the capacity by all to resist authority when it is abused.'[8] Symbol-making in the Gandhian mould is therefore a lonely path. It breaks free from the mainstream patronage that entraps and controls. It rejects the stereotype and its advantages. It acts as an agent provocateur, challenging society to turn its searchlight on itself. The symbolisation that is the result of this process of reflection is always improving, renewing and transforming reality into its better, purer and truer possibilities. It is a change that occurs from the bottom of society.

It is also a change that begins within the mind and conscience of the one who makes the symbols. A Gandhian communicator is therefore someone who is always striving to become a better, more authentic person and consequently, a more effective medium of communication. The inner confidence he or she possesses comes from transparency to self—the *sine qua non* for empowerment and perseverance through the usually long and arduous battle for a better world.

These six seemingly utopian principles were the foundation of Gandhi's process of symbolisation throughout the Swadeshi Movement. Indeed, the architectonic symbol of *purna swaraj* itself rested firmly on them. They typify, and in my reckoning, will continue to define the essence of Gandhian communication.

Yet, they were more than Gandhi's way of communicating, they were his *way of life*. Symbol and symboliser were one and the same—as he openly declared just four months before his assassination: 'My life is my message.'[9] All those who wished to follow him were invited to the same hard and uncompromising dedication to integrity and wholeness, a striving for symmetry in being and doing, in identity and self-expression. Gandhian symbolisation was never dualistic: the path *was* the goal.

Swadeshi in the pursuit of *swaraj* for all, beginning with the most underprivileged of India's outcastes was not merely a shrewd political ploy to drive out the British; it was Gandhi's whole being—his thinking, living, acting and his manner of presenting himself in public places. He epitomised this unity of purpose and action in his frail body, draped at the waist in simple hand-spun *khadi*. The unclothing of the Mahatma was his loudest cry on behalf of colonised humanity. It was the zenith of his search for sartorial significance. Here, in his own person, wedged between the clash of two great civilisations, he pursued an exceptional strategy to speak to an Empire that was too stubborn to listen, on behalf of the millions who spoke through their nakedness and their tears.

For those Indians who heeded Gandhi's cry, this 'clothing for liberation' was equivalent to putting one's life on the line. It meant giving up time, family and social privileges in the cause of moral duty. It involved subverting one's own inclinations before joining hands to subvert an empire. It required the willingness to lay down one's life in the hope that future generations might be free. The choice for *khadi* was no arbitrary fashion system; it was an option for perfect and uncompromising integrity.

Is it any wonder that Gandhi is so difficult to emulate today?

Shashi Tharoor, political scholar and acclaimed commentator on India, says it better:

> Mahatma Gandhi was the kind of person it is more convenient to forget. The principles he stood for and the way in which he asserted them are easier to admire than to follow. While he was alive he was impossible to ignore. Once he had gone he was impossible to imitate.[10]

Still, if we look behind the news headlines and images that feed our daily curiosity, we will encounter stories of people, symbol-makers from a variety of disciplines who have taken up the challenge of following in the teacher's footsteps. They may not be professed Gandhians, nor members of the many Gandhian institutes that dot the world. Yet, silently they try to be prophetic symbols: the change they wish to see in the world. In them, and through their work, the Mahatma continues to live on.[11]

Perhaps, now, in this globalised age, more than ever before, we need to examine more thoroughly the Gandhian process of symbolisation to guide our communication.

All conscientious symbol-makers—parents, educators, social workers, media professionals, intellectuals, activists, politicians and all people who have the responsibility to reconstruct and reinterpret reality for a better world—are invited to draw inspiration from Gandhi's 'experiments with truth'. Without his unitary vision, his spirit of introspection and his non-violent zeal we are in grave danger of constructing metaphors that perpetuate an exclusivist, competitive, parasitical and divided world.

Gandhi is more than a symbol-maker with a message that outlived his time and place. Without his inspiration we are consciously opting for a world rife with falsehood and violence. We are willingly choosing suicide.[12]

NOTES

1. In this chapter I wish to indicate the *approach* to Gandhian symbolisation. It is not my intention to spell out the details of each aspect on which a substantial amount of research and reflection is already available.
2. Tendulkar, *Mahatma*, 20.

3. It was Albert Einstein who eulogised Gandhi and set him up as a point of reference for the future: 'Generations to come will scarce believe that such a one as this ever in flesh and blood walked upon this earth.' Quotations from Einstein on Gandhi, *Gandhiserve*: http://streams.gandhiserve.org/einstein.html (5 July 2006). Arnold Toynbee's lesser known comment is equally significant: 'After Gandhi, humankind would expect its prophets to live in the slum of politics.' Cited by Ashis Nandy, 'The Ambivalence about Gandhi,' *Himal South Asian*, March–April 2006: http://www.himalmag.com/2006/march/reflections_3.html (11 October 2007).

4. Shashi Tharoor, *India, From Midnight to the Millennium* (New Delhi: Penguin Books, 2000), 22.

5. We distinguish 'objectively balanced scholarship' from lopsided, eclectic and subjective reductionism. Obviously, this calls for a careful selection of scholars who have proved their research and peer credibility.

6. Cf. the demanding letter Gandhi wrote to Manibhen Patel on his Silence Day, 21 May 1928: 'I want to see in you maturity, equanimity, contentment, discrimination, modesty, firmness, scrupulous regard for truth, earnestness, study and meditation. Without these yours will not be a life that becomes a virgin and dedicated social worker.' *CWMG*, vol. 36, 329.

7. R.K. Prabhu, (ed.), *Truth is God* (Ahmedabad: Navajivan Publishing House, 1955), 94.

8. A quotation of Gandhi cited in Chakravarty, *Mahatma Gandhi: The Great Communicator*, 397.

9. See 'Chronology,' 5 September 1947, in *CWMG*, vol. 89, 529.

10. Tharoor, *India, From Midnight to the Millennium*, 22.

11. I have made an attempt to list a few Gandhian symbol-makers from various disciplines across the world. The list is not exhaustive. See Appendix, 5, pp. 163–64.

12. Others have expressed similar sentiments: Dr M.L. King said, 'Gandhi was inevitable. If humanity is to progress, Gandhi is inescapable.... We may ignore him at our own risk' (quoted in Mark Hawthorne, 'Champions of Nonviolence,' http://www.mkgandhi-sarvodaya.org/articles/champions.htm (10 October 2009); B.R. Nanda warns his readers that today we can ignore Gandhi's words 'at our own peril' (B.R. Nanda, *In Search of Gandhi*, 145); John Paul II acclaimed Gandhi as the 'hero of humanity' and added: 'the peace and justice of which contemporary society has such great need will be achieved only along the path which was at the core of his teaching' (John Paul II, Address at Raj Ghat, 1 February 1986: http://www.vatican.va/holy_father/john_paul_ii/speeches/1986/february/documents/hf_jp-ii_spe_19860201_raj-ghat_en.html [8 December 2009].

Photographs and Images

Photographs and images of Gandhi's life, the Swadeshi Movement and imperialism in India are replete with significance in their semiological, performative and dramaturgical content. Following are examples of powerful visual communication through sartorial choices in a context of revolutionary change.

1. Mohandas at age seven, 1876
© *Vithalbhai Jhaveri/GandhiServe*

2. With elder brother, Laxmidas, 1886
© *Vithalbhai Jhaveri/GandhiServe*

3. In England, 1890
© *Vithalbhai Jhaveri/GandhiServe*

4. In South Africa, 1895
© *Vithalbhai Jhaveri/GandhiServe*

5. As a member of the Ambulance
Corps, South Africa, 1899
© *Vithalbhai Jhaveri/GandhiServe*

6. On a visit to London from
Johannesburg, 1906
© *Vithalbhai Jhaveri/GandhiServe*

7. In a mourning robe a *satyagraha*
campaign, S. Africa, 1913
© *Vithalbhai Jhaveri/GandhiServe*

8. In Kathiawadi dress, 1915
© *Vithalbhai Jhaveri/GandhiServe*

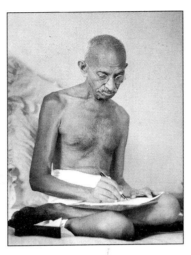

9. With the cap nicknamed, 'Gandhi *Topi*', Ahmedabad, 1920
© *Vithalbhai Jhaveri/GandhiServe*

10. In a 'loincloth', 1942
© *Kanu Gandhi/GandhiServe*

11. As a barefooted pilgrim of peace, Noakhali, 1946
© *Vithalbhai Jhaveri/GandhiServe*

12. The new *khadi*, hand-spun and woven flag drapes the Mahatma, 31 January 1948
© *Vithalbhai Jhaveri/GandhiServe*

13. Satyagrahis resisting the police at the Salt Satyagraha, 1930
© *Vithalbhai Jhaveri/GandhiServe*

14. A policeman confronts the woman with a bouquet of flowers, 1942
© *Vithalbhai Jhaveri/GandhiServe*

Performance management:

This page contrasts two performances of Gandhi: the young barrister in South Africa fully conscious of his self-importance, and the self-effacing Mahatma at a public meeting in India.

Comparative symbology:

Photographs on the next page reveal the sensitive nature of clothing choices in the interaction of two leaders with Gandhi. Nehru adopted *khadi*. Jinnah preferred to retain his Western attire.

15. In front of his office, Johannesburg, 1903
   © *Vithalbhai Jhaveri/GandhiServe*

16. At one of his prayer meetings, October 1947
   Courtesy: GandhiServe

17. Gandhi and Jinnah meet before talks with the Viceroy, 1942
Courtesy: The Hindu

18. Jawaharlal Nehru, his wife Kamala and daughter Indira, before and after they met Gandhi
Courtesy: Nehru Memorial Museum & Library

Mythologising reality:
The following two representations demonstrate how British imperial culture was preserved. The 1842 artist fixed the established perception of Indians as 'coolies' at the beck and call of their English lords; the second artist (p. 136) shocked his readers into imagining the parody of role reversals if the political co-opting of an increasing number of educated Indians around 1872 became the norm. The sarcasm reinforced the naturalised myth by ridiculing any attempt at change.

19. 'The Young Civilian's Toilet' by W. Tayler 1842
Courtesy: British Library Board, X.42, plate 1

20. 'The Baboo's Progress or What We Are Coming To!' from *The Indian Charivari*, 7 March 1873.
Courtesy: British Library Board, p. 3800 BG

Appendix

1. Gandhi's Fasts in India (1915–1948)

No.	Dates	Place	Reason	Results
1.	1918, 12–15 March	Ahmedabad	To protest against low wages and poor working conditions of mill workers.	Mill owners agreed to a 35% pay increase.
2.	1919, 13–15 April	Sabarmati	To atone for his 'Himalayan' miscalculation of launching civil disobedience.	Gandhi temporarily suspended the mass civil disobedience campaign.
3.	1921, 19–22 November	Bombay	To restore peace when riots erupted after visit of Prince of Wales.	Peace restored.
4.	1922, 12–16 February	Bardoli	To protest against violence, especially the Chauri Chaura riots.	Gandhi suspended indefinitely the mass civil disobedience campaign.
5.	1924, 17 September–7 October	M. Ali's house, Delhi	The 'Great' Fast to protest Hindu–Muslim rioting.	Conference of religious leaders convened on 26 September, and it urged communal unity.
6.	1925, 24–30 November	Sabarmati	To atone for lapses in the behaviour of ashram members.	Dramatised that social regeneration requires personal purity.

(Contd.)

(Contd.)

No.	Dates	Place	Reason	Results
7.	1932, 20–26 September	Yervada Prison, Poona	To protest against Prime Minister MacDonald's Electorate Award to Untouchables; Gandhi feared perpetuation of casteism.	Yervada Pact (Poona Pact) agreed: 'Henceforth no one is to be regarded as Untouchable…'
8.	1932, 22 December	Yervada Prison, Poona	To sympathise with a fellow prisoner's desire to do scavenger's work.	Authorities reversed their decision; Appasaheb Patwardhan is allowed to work.
9.	1933, 8–29 May	Poona	For 'self-purification' and to urge greater efforts for *Harijans*.	Many leaders, including Tagore, Smuts and Rajagopalachari feared for his life.
10.	1933, 16–23 August	Yervada Prison	To protest against his imprisonment and denial of right to do menial work.	Released from prison on 23 August because the British feared for his life.
11.	1934, 7–13 August	Wardha	To atone for violence at a public meeting in Ajmer.	Gandhi wrote that the fast had for him 'unestimable' spiritual value.
12.	1939, 3–7 March	Rajkot	To protest against a local ruler's failure to abide by a reforms agreement.	Won the Viceroy's intervention; later rejected the fast for being coercive.
13.	1943, 10 February–3 March	Aga Khan Palace, Poona	To protest against the Viceroy's charge that Gandhi and Congress caused violence.	Gandhi nearly died; three members of Viceroy's Executive Committee resigned.
14.	1947, 1–4 September	Calcutta	To protest against communal violence which shook India following partition.	Calm returned to Calcutta: many weapons turned in.
15.	1948, 13–18 January	Delhi	Issued seven demands on behalf of Muslims.	All demands were met; Commission established to protect Muslims' rights.

Sources: Merriam, 'Symbolic Action in India', 294 and Goswami, *Chronology*, 241.

2. The Effect of Gandhi's Fasts

To understand the impact of Gandhi's fast on the population, we cite two examples:

The epic fast of 1932

This fast-unto-death was observed by Gandhi when he heard that the British Prime Minister Ramsey MacDonald had awarded separate electorates to Untouchables. He was against the move for fear that it would fragment Indian politics into communally based antipathies. In a widely circulated press release Gandhi made it abundantly clear that his fast was not directed against the separate electorates alone but against the *prevailing practice of untouchability itself.* Perhaps he found this the right moment to demand the attention of the caste Hindus who earlier did not take his repeated pleas to ban untouchability seriously.[1] He was firm in his resolve as expressed in his statement: 'No patched-up agreement between caste Hindus and rival depressed class leaders will answer the purpose. The agreement to be valid has to be real. If the Hindu mass mind is not yet prepared to banish untouchability root and branch, it must sacrifice me without the slightest hesitation.'[2]

There followed a nation-wide response. On the day of the fast, the Kalighat Temple of Calcutta and the Ram Mandir of Benaras—the citadels of Hindu orthodoxy—were thrown open. In Bombay, where a nationalist women's organisation conducted a poll of worshippers in front of seven big temples, 247,976 voted for and 445 against the admission of *harijan*s. Thousands of prominent Hindu women accepted food from the hands of the Untouchables, and at the Benaras Hindu University, the principal and scores of Brahmins dined publicly with them. Such scenes were repeated in many villages and cities. Many Hindus took pledges not to practise untouchability themselves or to allow it to be practised in their families.[3]

As his physical condition deteriorated, Hindu leaders negotiated with Ambedkar in order to reach a compromise. The decision temporarily arrived at was to allot political seats for untouchables instead of granting them separate electoral status. The Poona Pact was thus signed and Gandhi ended his fast six days later. But the changes triggered a deep moral stirring in the Hindu psyche in many parts of India. Untouchability was now at the top of the national agenda although Gandhi and his followers were unable to keep up the pressure in the years that followed.

The fast of 1943

Another example of the powerful communicative force behind Gandhi's fasting was the three-week fast of 1943. He undertook the fast to protest against Viceroy Linlithgow's charge that he and the Congress Party bore responsibility for the violence surrounding the 'Quit India' campaign. The Government had expected this response from Gandhi and it was obdurate. It decided to 'effectively limit his freedom to communicate with the outside world'.[4] Gandhi and the Congress were presented in newspapers as saboteurs of the Allied struggle against Japan. There were attempts to erase him from political life by excluding his photographs and even a mention of his name from the Press. Moreover, the Government took a risk it had never taken before—it was ready to let Gandhi die. A terse one-sentence announcement was prepared to be released in the event of his death: 'The Government of India regrets to announce that Mr. Gandhi died while in detention at Poona at __hrs on ____ from collapse/heart failure following a self imposed fast.'[5]

Yet the frustration faced by the authorities who were already preoccupied with the war in Europe was aggravated by the foreboding spectre of a cataclysmic rebellion all over India should Gandhi die during the fast. It would be a historical embarrassment in the eyes of the world. The emotional upheaval in the country increased as doctor's bulletins grew gloomier. The Wartime Cabinet documents[6] show that ministers argued fiercely about the consequences of allowing Gandhi to die while interned at their hands during the Second World War.[7] Three members of the Viceroy's Executive Committee resigned. Leaders of various parties, whatever their other differences, united in appeals to the Government to release him and save his life. But the Viceroy, backed by the Prime Minister, Mr Winston Churchill, did not budge an inch. The Viceroy described the fast as 'political blackmail'. Churchill was incensed by the prospect of handing Gandhi a moral victory.[8] He insisted that any move should be portrayed as a victory for the British authorities. The result was that Gandhi nearly died. He ended his fast on 3 March 1943. He was finally released in 1944.

The people of India had woken up in a way that went beyond even Gandhi's control. In imprisoning Gandhi and repudiating his fast, the Government did more harm to itself. It confined the one man who could control the violence that was waiting to explode in the face of British defiance.

3. A Ten-year Sample of Gandhi's Journeys (1915–1925)

Year	Names of Places Visited as Mentioned in the Chronology
1915	Bombay, Ahmedabad, Poona, Calcutta, Rangoon, Haridwar, Delhi, Madras
1916	Surat, Madras, Hyderabad, Madras, Ahmedabad, Allahabad, Lucknow, Bombay
1917	Karachi, Calcutta, Patna, Champaran district, Ranchi, Allahabad, Godhra, Viramgam, Muzaffarpur, Delhi, Aligarh, Calcutta
1918	Ahmedabad, Kheda, Nadiad, Delhi, Bombay, *Suffers ill health from 11 August 1918 to February 1919*
1919	Ahmedabad, Delhi, Bombay, Madras, Bezwada, Lahore, Amritsar
1920	Ahmedabad, Delhi, Lahore, tour of Punjab, Bombay, Jullundur, Amritsar, Lahore, Rawalpindi, Gujarkhan, Hyderabad, Madras, Mangalore, Calcutta, Surat, Rohtak, Moradabad, Satara, Agra, Benares, Allahabad, Phulwari Shariff, Patna, Arrah, Muzaffarpur, Bettiah, Monghyr, Nagpur
1921	Ahmedabad, Nadiad, Vadtal, Calcutta, Patna, Banaras, Delhi, Bhiwani, Rohtak, Lucknow, Nankana Sahib, Bombay, Cuttack, Vijayanagaram, Bezwada, Cocanada, Nellore, Madras, Jalol, Surat, Karachi, Kapadvanj, Kathlal, Allahabad, Simla, Barsi, Samod, Kanpur, Chittagong, Kumbakonam, Madura, Lahore
1922	Bombay, Ahmedabad, Bardoli, Delhi, *Arrested on 10 March and taken to Sabarmati Jail, then to Yervada Prison to serve term of six years*
1923	*Imprisoned in Yervada jail*
1924	*Released on February 4.* Poona, Bombay, Ahmedabad, Delhi, Amritsar, Lahore, Rawalpindi, Belgaum
1925	Bhavnagar, Ahmedabad, Petlad, Delhi, Rawalpindi, Palej, Kathiawar tour, Rajkot, Madras, Vykom, Allepey, Varkalai, Trivandrum, Parur, Trichur, Cochin, Bombay, Supa, Navsari, Madhav Bagh, Calcutta, Faridpur, Chandernagore, tour of East Bengal, Dacca, Naokhali, Comilla, Vikrampur, Shyampur, Darjeeling, Jalpaiguri, Barisal, Khulna, Kidderpore, Behrampur, Jamshedpur, Purulia, Patna, Khagaul, Bikram, Bhagalpur, Benares, Lucknow, Dwarka, Bhuj, Dholka, Wardha

The above list of places traces the itinerary of Gandhi on a yearly basis but does not repeat the names of sites already visited earlier in the year. The list may not be exhaustive nor accurate.[9]

4. Gandhi's Letter-writing in Conflict

Here are three examples of Gandhi's letter-writing in three different conflict situations:

A. A letter to a certain Gangaramji:[10]
February 21, 1921
Dear Gangaramji,
This is what is averred against you:

1. You and Mr. Gaurishanker have misappropriated monies.
2. Your schools are mostly bogus.
3. You have a bogus committee.
4. You have published no accounts.
5. You do not collect from those who are said to benefit by your schools.
6. You were charged with misappropriation, but acquitted. The public belief is that the charge was not ill-founded.
7. You are keeping a woman by whom you have children.

There seems to be strong ground for believing these things.
If you desire an inquiry, I would ask some of the friends you mention to conduct the inquiry.

Yours sincerely,
M.K. Gandhi

B. A reply to a 'Letter to the Editor' published in *Navajivan*:[11]
Q. *You say you are not a dictator. Have you ever been guided by any leader to the smallest extent? Even in the Subjects Committee, you remained adamant as a rock. At times you ask us to follow the voice of our conscience; why are you, then, struggling so hard to canvass support for your view?*
A. I certainly believe that I am not a dictator. Not only that, there is not even a trace of dictatorship in me, since the way that I have embraced is that of service. I have often been guided in the past by many leaders and still am. In the Subjects Committee meetings, I yielded on many points, at Calcutta as also at Nagpur. But this indeed is true, that in matters of conscience I am uncompromising. Nobody can make me yield. I, therefore, tolerate the charge of being a dictator. Though I ask people to obey the voice of their conscience, everyone has the right to convince others by argument. The conscience in us

likes to go to sleep. It requires to be aroused from time to time, and that is the worthiest effort for man. Helping one another to break our chains is the truest service.

C. As an example of frank letter-writing to dignitaries see the excerpt from the famous letter to Lord Irwin, dated 2 March 1930.[12] Gandhi informs him of his plan to launch civil disobedience through the Salt March to Dandi. In the earlier part of the letter he explains that he means no harm to Englishmen although he believes the British rule in India is a curse. He gives his reasons for his opinion and cites examples of how India has been politically reduced to serfdom and has been robbed of the foundations of its culture. His firm, well-studied presentation of facts with candid directness and without arrogance or anger is a masterpiece in Gandhian conflict resolution, non-violent strategy and persuasive letter-writing.

5. In the Footsteps of Gandhi

Gandhian theory and praxis have influenced thinkers and activists from various disciplines. Below I present a few examples:

- *Agriculture:* M.S. Swaminathan, Paul Keene, Miguel Altieri
- *Architecture:* Laurie Baker, Charles Correa
- *Business:* N.R. Narayana Murthy, Verghese Kurien
- *Communication and Journalism:* Sean McBride, P. Sainath, E. Galeano
- *Ecology and Nuclear Disarmament:* Vandana Shiva, Arne Naess, Barry Commoner, Helen Caldicott, Caucus Kucinich
- *Economics:* John K. Galbraith, E. Schumacher, Muhammad Yunus
- *Education:* Maria Montessori, Danilo Dolci, Mark Juergensmeyer
- *International Organisations:* The United Nations, Greenpeace International, Amnesty International
- *Literature:* Nadine Gordimer, Arundhati Roy, Gary Snyder
- *Management:* Stephen Covey
- *Movements for Justice and Peace:* Vinobha Bhave, Cesar Estrada Chavez, A.T. Ariyaratne, Chandi Prasad Bhatt, Adolfo Pérez Esquivel, Ela Bhatt, Baba Amte, Aruna Roy, Medha Patkar, Andrea Riccardi, Arvind Kejriwal

- *Music:* Joan Baez, Carlos Santana
- *Peace Research:* Johan Galtung, Robert E. Klitgaard, Giuliano Pontara, Thomas Weber
- *Politics:* Martin Luther King, Chidambaram Subramaniam, Nelson Mandela, Aung San Suu Kyi, Lech Walesa, Kofi Annan
- *Poltical Science:* Noam Chomsky, Gene Sharp, Jean-Marie Muller
- *Psychology:* Erik H. Erikson, Albert Ellis, Linden L. Nelson, Mubarak Awad
- *Religion:* Thich Nhat Hanh, Helder Camara, Dalai Lama, Desmond Tutu, Preah Maha Ghosinanda, Thomas Merton, Eknath Easwaran, Alessandro Zanotelli, Henri Nouwen, David Steindl-Rast
- *Religious Tolerance/Communal Harmony:* Asghar Ali Engineer, Teesta Setalvad, Cedric Prakash
- *Science:* Albert Einstein, Carl Sagan, Fang Lizhi

In 1981, 53 Nobel Laureates signed their 'Manifesto of Nobel Prize Recipients' in which they made explicit mention of Gandhi as an example for world peace (although, Gandhi never received a Nobel Prize[13]).

In 2005, a unique study of 67 countries, in which transitions from authoritarianism to democratic rule occurred, was conducted by international thinktank Freedom House. The transitions that took place after World War II reveal that far more often than is generally understood, *the change agent is broad-based, non-violent civic resistance,* which employs tactics such as boycotts, mass protests, blockades, strikes and civil disobedience to de-legitimate authoritarian rulers and erode their sources of support, including the loyalty of their armed defenders.[14]

The United Nations General Assembly unanimously adopted a resolution on 15 June 2007 to observe and celebrate annually Mahatma Gandhi's birthday, 2 October, as the International Day of Non-violence. The resolution was piloted by India and was co-sponsored by 142 countries.[15]

Notes

1. Gandhi consistently sought to abolish untouchability because, among other things, it was counterproductive to obtaining *swaraj*. It was hypocritical of the majority Hindu population to demand liberty from the British while still subjugating the low castes and outcasts of Hindu society. In seeking separate electorates the

untouchables were demanding a complete break from Hinduism. Gandhi had warned orthodox Hindus about this separation but they did not heed.

2. Ambedkar, *What Congress and Gandhi have Done*, 77.
3. Parekh, *Colonialism*, 261.
4. Nicholas Mansergh (ed.), *The Transfer of Power*, 1942–1947, III, (London: Her Majesty's Stationery Office, 1971), 451; quoted by Allen H. Merriam, 'Symbolic Action in India, Gandhi's Nonverbal Persuasion', *Quarterly Journal of Speech*, 61, Washington DC, NCA, October, 1975, 295.
5. Merriam, *Symbolic Action in India*, 296.
6. Recorded in shorthand by Sir Norman Brook, the deputy cabinet secretary.
7. 'Demands to Let Gandhi Die on Hunger Strike,' *Timesonline*, 1 January 2006, http://www.timesonline.co.uk/article/0,2087-1965609,00.html (5 January 2006).
8. *Ibid.* See also Churchill's boast on how he made Gandhi change his mind in Bamber Gascoigne, 'Mahatma Gandhi (1869–1948),' *Books and Writers*: http://www.kirjasto.sci.fi/gandhi.htm (6 December 2005).
9. Cf. Goswami (ed.), *Mahatma Gandhi, A Chronology*, (Delhi: Publications Division, Government of India, 1971).
10. *CWMG*, vol. 19 377.
11. *CWMG*, vol. 19 298.
12. For the complete letter see *CWMG*, vol. 43 2–8.
13. Cf. Thomas Weber, *Gandhi, Gandhism and the Gandhians* (New Delhi: Roli Books, 2006), 95–120.
14. Adrian Karatnycky and Peter Ackerman, *How Freedom is Won: From Civic Resistance to Durable Democracy* (New York: Freedom House, 2005), 4 (emphasis mine). Web version: http://www.freedomhouse.org/uploads/special_report/29.pdf (24 September 2007).
15. 'Mahatma Gandhi's Teachings Reflect UN Ideals Says UN Chief,' *United Nations Radio News Service*, 2 October 2007, http://www.un.org/radio/news/html/13506.html (12 October 2007).

Glossary[1]

Ahimsa: non-violence

Atman: soul

Ashram: a hermitage, traditionally the abode of Hindu sages amidst nature

Avatar: an incarnation of the divine being (Vishnu) into the mortal realm

Bania: a trader, the caste group to which M. K. Gandhi's family belonged

Bhagavad Gita: 'The Song of the Lord', one of Hinduism's sacred books

Chakra: wheel; on the Indian flag the wheel is that of Emperor Ashoka

Charkha: spinning wheel

Darbar, Durbar: the official reception of a native ruler or British viceroy

Darshan: to see a deity or saint and thereby receive blessings

Dharma: righteousness, the Divine Plan

Dhoti: cloth draped around the lower part of the male, from waist to feet

Harijan: 'Children of God', a name Gandhi gave the Dalits and his newspaper started in 1933

Hartal: general strike

Himsa: violence

Kama: desire

Karma: action

Khadi, Khaddar: cloth made from home-spun yarn

Mahatma: great soul

Moksha: eternal bliss, liberation of the soul from the cycle of rebirths

Mauna: silence

Navajivan: 'New Life', the title of Gandhi's newspaper started in 1919

Nishkama-karma: action-without-desire

Purna Swaraj: freedom from all personal and social evils
Ramarajya: the kingdom of God
Rishi: a seer or sage who was inspired to write the Vedic hymns
Sanyasi: one engaged in the discipline of *sanyas*
Sanyas: the renunciation of desire and attachment
Sarvodaya: compassion towards all
Saree/Sari: draped clothing worn by women of India
Sat: Truth/Being
Satya: truthfulness
Satyagraha: Truth-force
Satyagrahi: a volunteer dedicated to *satyagraha*
Swadesh: of one's own country; *swadeshi* (adj.) as in '*swadeshi* cloth'
Swaraj: self-rule, home-rule, concretely: Independence from British rule
Takhposh: low wooden settee
Topi: a cap, usually referred to as the Gandhian cap
Upavas: fasting
Varnavyavastha: the Caste System
Vedas: the oldest scriptures of Hinduism, c. 2500 and 600 B.C.
Yajna/Yagna: ritual sacrifice

Numerical Units: 1 lakh = 100,000; 1 crore = 10,000,000
Value of the Rupee in 1893: Re 1 = 15 pence; £1 = Rs 15.[2]

Notes

1. Most words are in the singular. The plural 's' is added where appropriate.
2. The Rupee exchange rate is from B.E. Dadachanji, *History of Indian Currency and Exchange* (Bombay: D.B. Taraporevala Sons & Co., 1934), 15.

Select Bibliography

The bibliography is divided into two sections to facilitate identification of sources. Books, articles and websites concerning Gandhi and the Swadeshi Movement are in Section A. References to Communication Theories are found in Section B.

A. Gandhi and the Swadeshi Revolution

Andrews, Charles F. *Mahatma Gandhi: His Life and Ideas.* Mumbai: Jaico Publishing House, 2005.

Arya, P.P. and B.B. Tandon, ed. *Multinationals versus Swadeshi Today.* New Delhi: Deep and Deep Publications, 1999.

Baines, Edward. *History of the Cotton Manufacture in Great Britain: A Description of the Great Mechanical Inventions.* London: H. Fisher, R, Fisher and P. Jackson, 1835.

Bakker J.I. *Towards a Just Civilization: The Gandhian Perspective on Human Rights and Development,* Toronto: Canadian Scholars' Press, 1993. http://www.uoguelph. ca/~vincent/hbakker/work/toward_a_just_civilization.htm (1 May 2005).

Bakshi, S.R. *Gandhi and the Ideology of Swadeshi.* New Delhi: Reliance Publishing House, 1987.

Bayly, C. 'The Origins of *Swadeshi* (Home Industry): Cloth and Indian Society, 1700–1930.' In *The Social Life of Things,* edited by Arjun Appadorai, 285–321. Cambridge: Cambridge University Press, 1986.

———. *The Raj: India and the British 1600–1947.* London: National Portrait Gallery, 1990.

Bean, Susan. 'Gandhi and Khadi, Fabric of Independence.' In *Cloth and Human Experience,* edited by Annette Weiner and Jane Schneider, 355–76. Washington: Smitsonian Books, 1989.

Bharathi, K.S. 'Swadeshi and Globalisation.' *Gandhi Marg,* April–June (2005): 59–73.

Bhattacharya, Bhabani. *Gandhi the Writer.* New Delhi: National Book Trust, (1969) 2002.

Bhattacharyya, Sailendra Nath. *Mahatma Gandhi the Journalist.* Bombay: Asia Publishing House, 1965.

Bligh M.C. and J.L. Robinson. 'Different Routes to Charisma and Taking the Road Less Travelled: An Analysis of Gandhi's Rhetorical Leadership.' *Cross-Cultural*

Leadership and Management Studies, no. 1, 109–25 (2004), www.cgu.edu/include/flmspr04.pdf (24 May 2005).

Bode, Robert. 'Gandhi's Theory of Nonviolent Communication.' *Gandhi Marg,* April–June (1994): 7–29.

Brown, Judith. *Gandhi: Prisoner of Hope.* London: Yale University Press, 1989.

Chakravarty, Nikhil. 'Mahatma Gandhi: The Great Communicator.' *Gandhi Marg,* January–March (1995): 389–97.

Chamberlain, Joseph. 'The British Viewpoint on Imperialism—Speech to the Royal Colonial Institute, March 31, 1897', http://web.jjay.cuny.edu/~jobrien/reference/ob70.html (20 September 2007).

Chambers, Robert. *Rural Development: Putting the Last First.* London: Longman, 1983.

Chandra, Bipin. *Freedom Struggle.* New Delhi: National Book Trust, 1972.

———. *India's Struggle for Independence.* New Delhi: Penguin Books, 1989.

Chatterjee, Parta. *The Nation and Its Fragments: Colonial and Postcolonial Histories.* New Delhi: Oxford University Press, 2001.

———. ed. *Wages of Freedom: Fifty Years of the Indian Nation-State.* Delhi: Oxford University Press, 1998.

Chaudhuri, N.C. *Culture in the Vanity Bag: Clothing and Adornment in Passing and Abiding India.* Bombay: Jaico Publishing House, 1976.

Chaudhuri, Ranjit. 'Gandhi in Search of Gandhi: A Study of His Autobiography.' *Gandhi Marg* 21(1999): 313–23.

Cohn, Bernard S. *Colonialism and Its Forms of Knowledge—The British in India.* New Jersey: Princeton University Press, 1996.

———. 'Cloth, Clothes and Colonialism: India in the Nineteenth Century.' In *Cloth and Human Experience,* edited by Annette Weiner and Jane Schneider, 303–53. Washington: Smitsonian Books, 1989.

Coomaraswamy, Ananda. *Art and Swadeshi.* Delhi: Munshiram Manoharlal, 1994.

Copley, Antony. *Gandhi against the Tide.* Delhi: Oxford University Press, 1987.

Deluca, Anthony R. *Gandhi, Mao, Mandela, and Gorbachev: Studies in Personality, Power, and Politics.* Westport, CT: Praeger Publishers, 2000.

Dirks, Nicholas. *Castes of Mind: Colonialism and the Making of Modern India.* New Jersey: Princeton University Press, 2001.

Diwan, Romesh. 'Mahatma Gandhi, Amartya Sen, and Poverty.' *Gandhi Marg* 20 (1999): 421–43.

Erikson, Eric. *Gandhi's Truth: On the Origins of Militant Nonviolence.* New York: Norton, 1969.

Fischer, Louis. *The Life of Mahatma Gandhi.* New York: HarperCollins Publishers, (1951) 1997.

Gandhi, M.K. *An Autobiography* or *The Story of My Experiments with Truth.* Ahmedabad: Navajivan, (1927) 2005.

———. *Collected Works of Mahatma Gandhi, Vols 1–90.* New Delhi: Publications Division, Government of India, 1994.

———. *Constructive Programme, Its Meaning and Place.* Ahmedabad: Navajivan Publishing House, (1941) 2005.

———. *Hind Swaraj and Other Writings,* edited by Anthony J. Parel. New Delhi: Foundation Books, 2004.

Gandhi, M.K. *Satyagraha in South Africa*. Ahmedabad: Navajivan, 1928; Yann, Forget. http://www.forget-me.net/en/Gandhi/satyagraha.pdf (12 April 2007).

———. *Khadi: Why and How,* edited by Bharatan Kumarappa. Ahmedabad: Navajivan, 1955.

———. *Making of a Great Communicator, Gandhi*. Edited by Bharati Narasimhan. New Delhi: National Media Centre, 1997.

———. *Swaraj Through Charkha*. Edited by Kanu Gandhi. Sevagram: All India Spinners' Association, 1945.

Gandhi, Rajmohan. *The Good Boatman: A Portrait of Gandhi*. New Delhi: Penguin Books, 1997.

Gardner Howard. *Creating Minds: An Anatomy of Creativity Seen Through the Lives of Freud, Einstein, Picasso, Stravinsky, Eliot, Graham, and Gandhi*. New York: Basic Books, 1994.

Geeta, V., ed. *Soul Force: Gandhi's Writings on Peace*. Chennai: Tara Publishing, 2004.

Gonsalves, Peter. '"Half-naked Fakir", The Story of Gandhi's Personal Search for Sartorial Integrity.' *Gandhi Marg* 31 (2009): 5–30.

Goswami, K.P. *Mahatma Gandhi—A Chronology*. Delhi: Publications Division, Government of India, 1971.

Goswami, Manu. *Producing India: From Colonial Economy to National Space*. New York: University of Chicago Press, 2004.

Government Of India. *The Khadi Industry*. Delhi: Publications Division, 1962.

Guha, Ramachandra. 'Churchill and Gandhi.' *The Hindu*, 19 June 2005. http://www.hindu.com/mag/2005/06/19/stories/2005061900060300.htm (4 September 2007).

———. 'A Father Betrayed.' *The Guardian*, 14 August 2007. http://www.guardian.co.uk/india/story/0,,2148286,00.html (25 September 2007).

Guha, Ranajit, ed. *A Subaltern Studies Reader 1986–1995*. Delhi: Oxford University Press, 1998.

Habib, Irfan. *Indian Economy 1858–1914* (A People's History of India, No. 28). New Delhi: Aligarh Historians Society, Tulika Books, 2006.

Harzinski, Rachael. 'A Tale of two Cloths: The Transition from Wool to Cotton Undergarments in England during the Victorian Age.' Eastern Illinois University website: http://www.eiu.edu/%7ehistoria/2006/harzinski2006.pdf (4 July 2006).

Imhasly, Bernard, Schmidt, Christian, Bauer Manuel, Gestaltung Winterthur, Prill Satz Tania and Vieceli Alberto. *Khadi—Textile of India*. Zürich: Kontrast AG, 2002.

Ishii, Kazuya. 'The Socioeconomic Thoughts of Mahatma Gandhi: As an Origin of Alternative Development.' *Review of Social Economy* 59(2001): 297–312.

Jordens, J.T.F. *Gandhi's Religion: A Homespun Shawl*. New York: Palgrave, 1998.

Joshi, Nandini. *Development without Destruction, Economics of the Spinning Wheel*. Ahmedabad: Navajivan, 1992.

Juergensmeyer, Mark. *Fighting with Gandhi: A Step-by-Step Strategy for Resolving Everyday Conflicts*. San Francisco: Harper & Row Publishers, 1984.

———. *Gandhi's Way: A Handbook of Conflict Resolution*. Berkeley: University of California Press, 2002.

Kaushik, Asha. *Politics, Symbols and Political Theory—Rethinking Gandhi*. New Delhi: Rawat Publications, 2001.

Keay, John. *The Honourable Company: A History of the English East India Company.* New York: HarperCollins, 1993.

Kripalani, J.B. *Gandhi, His Life and Thought.* Delhi: Publications Division, Government of India, 1970.

Kripalani, Krishna. *Gandhi: A Life.* New Delhi: National Book Trust, 1982.

Kumar, Keval. 'Gandhi's Ideological Clothing', *Media Development* 31, no. 4(1984): 19–21.

———. 'Mahatma Gandhi as a Mass Communicator.' In *Communicating the Gospel Today*, edited by Gnana Robinson, 171–97. Madurai: Tamilnadu Theological Seminary, 1986.

Kumar, Sudhir. 'Towards a Gandhian Approach to Literature.' *Gandhi Marg* 22 (2000): 319–30.

Kumarappa, J.C. *Economy of Permanence.* Varanasi: Sarva Seva Sangh Prakashan, 1947.

Kuruvachira, J. *Hindu Nationalists of Modern India—A Critical Study of the Intellectual Genealogy of Hindutva.* Delhi: Media House, 2005.

Lange, Matthew. 'Colonialism and Development: A Comparative Analysis of Spanish and British Colonies.' *AJS* 111 (2006): 1412–62.

Lannoy, Richard. *The Speaking Tree: A Study of Indian Culture and Society.* New Delhi: Oxford University Press, 1999.

Lemire, Beverly. *Fashion's Favourite: The Cotton Trade and the Consumer in Britain, 1660–1800.* Oxford: Oxford University Press, 1991.

Lisa, Trivedi. *Clothing Gandhi's Nation—Homespun and Modern India.* Bloomington: Indiana University Press, 2007.

Logan, Frenise A. 'India's Loss of the British Cotton Market after 1865.' *The Journal of Southern History* 31(1965): 40–50.

Mack, Phyllis. 'Feminine Behavior and Radical Action: Franciscans, Quakers, and the Followers of Gandhi.' *Signs* 11 (1986): 457–77.

Mandela, Nelson. 'Gandhi the Prisoner.' In *Mahatma Gandhi: 125 Years*, edited by B.R. Nanda. New Delhi: Indian Council for Cultural Relations, 1995; also African National Congress website: http://www.anc.org.za/ancdocs/history/people/gandhi/man-gan.html (27 May 2006).

Markovits, Claude. *The Un-Gandhian Gandhi, The Life and Afterlife of the Mahatma.* Delhi: Permanent Black, 2004.

Mehta, Ved. *Mahatma Gandhi and His Apostles.* New Delhi: Indian Book Company, 1976.

Merriam, Allen H. 'Symbolic Action in India: Gandhi's Nonverbal Persuasion.' *Quarterly Journal of Speech* 61 (1975): 290–306.

Munshi, K.M. *Gujarati and its Literature.* Bombay: Longmans Green & Co., 1935.

Nanda, B. R. *Gandhi and His Critics.* Oxford: Oxford University Press, 1996.

———. *In Search of Gandhi, Essays and Reflections.* New Delhi: Oxford University Press, 2002.

———. *Mahatma Gandhi—A Biography.* New Delhi: Oxford University Press, 2002.

———. *The Making of A Nation, India's Road to Independence.* New Delhi: Harper Collins Publishers, 1998.

Nandy, Ashish. 'From Outside the Imperium: Gandhi's Cultural Critique of the West.' In *Contemporary Crisis and Gandhi*, edited by Ramashray Roy, 89–126. Delhi: Discovery Publishing House, 1986.

Naess, Arne. 'Gandhian Nonviolent Verbal Communication: The Necessity of Training.' *Gandhi Marg,* April–June (2005): 89–99.

Nehru Jawaharlal. *An Autobiography.* New Delhi: Penguin Books, 2004.

———. *The Discovery of India.* New Delhi: Penguin Books, 2004.

———. *Mahatma Gandhi, Reflection on his Personality and Teachings.* Bombay: Bharatiya Vidya Bhavan, 1989.

Oommen, T.K. *Citizenship and National Identity: From Colonialism to Globalism.* New Delhi: Sage Publications, 1997.

Paige, Glenn D. *To Nonviolent Political Science: From Seasons of Violence.* Honolulu: Center for Global Nonkilling, 2009, 133–56.

Pandey, Janardan, ed. *Gandhi and Voluntary Organizations.* Bhagalpur: M. D. Publications, 1998.

Panditrao, Yashwant. *Cottage and Village Industries in the Indian Economy.* Mumbai: Mani Bhavan Gandhi Sangrahalaya, 2003.

Panini, M.N. 'Caste, Race and Human Rights.' In *Caste, Race and Discrimination,* edited by Sukhadeo Thorat and Umakant, 176–78. Jaipur: Rawat Publications, 2004.

Parekh, Bhikhu. *Colonialism, Tradition and Reform: An Analysis of Gandhi's Political Discourse.* New Delhi: Sage Publications, 1999.

———. *Gandhi's Political Philosophy: A Critical Examination.* Notre Dame: University of Notre Dame Press, 1989.

Parel, Anthony J., ed. *Gandhi, Freedom, and Self-rule.* Oxford: Lexington Books, 2000.

———. *Gandhi's Philosophy and the Quest for Harmony.* New York: Cambridge University Press, 2006.

Patil, V.T. *Studies on Gandhi.* New Delhi: Sterling Press, 1983.

Polak, Henry, Brailsford, Henry Noel and Pethik-Lawrence, Lord. *Mahatma Gandhi.* London: Odhams Press, 1949.

Polak, Millie. *Mr. Gandhi: The Man.* Bombay: Vora, 1950.

Prabhu, R.K. and RAO, U.R. *The Mind of Mahatma Gandhi.* Ahmedabad: Navajivan Publishing House, (1945) 2002.

Puri, Rashmi-Sudha. 'Gandhi's *Maun*: Springs of Strength.' *Gandhi Marg* 23 (2002), 415–28.

Pyarelal. *Mahatma Gandhi: The Early Phase.* Allahabad: Navajivan, 1965.

———. *Mahatma Gandhi: The Last Phase (Part I, 1956 & Part II, 1958).* Allahabad: Navajivan, 1956 and 1958.

Qadir, Abdul. 'A Statesman in Beggar's Garb.' In *Mahatma Gandhi—Essays and Reflections on his Life and Work,* edited by Radhakrishnan, 240–41. Mumbai: Jaico Publishing House, 2004.

Radhakrishnan, Sarvepalli. *Mahatma Gandhi—Essays and Reflections on his Life and Work.* Mumbai: Jaico Publishing House, 2004.

Ramagundam, Rahul. *Gandhi's Khadi: A History of Contention and Conciliation.* Hyderabad: Orient Longman Private Limited, 2008.

Robins, Nick. *The Corporation that Changed the World.* Hyderabad: Orient Longman, 2006.

Roy, Ramashray, ed. *Contemporary Crisis and Gandhi.* Delhi: Discovery Publishing House, 1986.

Roy, Ramashray. *Gandhi: Soundings in Political Philosophy.* Delhi: Chanakya Publications, 1984.

Roy, Ramashray. *Self and Society: A Study of Gandhian Thought*. New Delhi: Sage Publications, 1984.

Rothermund, Indira. 'The Gandhian Pattern of Mass Communication.' *Gandhi Marg*, March (1987): 712–19.

Rudolph, Susanne Hoeber and Lloyd I Rudolph. *Gandhi, The Traditional Roots of Charisma*. Chicago: University of Chicago Press, 1983.

———. *Postmodern Gandhi and Other Essays: Gandhi in the World and at Home*. Chicago: University of Chicago Press, 2006.

Ruhe, Peter. *Gandhi: A Photo Biography*. London: Phaidon Press, 2001.

Sahasrabudhey, Sunil. 'On Cultural Alienation.' *Gandhi Marg*, September (1986): 327–47.

Sarkar, Sumit. *Writing Social History*. Delhi: Oxford University Press, 1997.

Scalmer, Sean. 'Globalising Gandhi: Processes, Transformations, Questions.' In *Embodying Non-Violence in the World: Historicising Gandhi's Global Legacy*, edited by Debjani Ganguly and John Docker, 141–62. New Delhi: Orient Longman, 2007.

Schumacher, E.F. *Small is Beautiful, Economics as if People Mattered*. New York: Perennial Library/Harper and Row, 1973.

Sen, Amartya. *Choice of Techniques*, Oxford: Basil Blackwell, 1960.

———. *The Argumentative Indian*. London: Penguin Books, 2005.

Sen, Nabendu. *India in the International Economy 1858–1913. Some Aspects of Trade and Finance*. Calcutta: Orient Longman, 1992.

Sen, Sudipta. *Empire of Free Trade: The East India Company and the Making of the Colonial Marketplace*. Philadelphia: University of Pennsylvania Press, 1998.

Sharma, Sunil, ed. *Journalist Gandhi—Selected Writings of Gandhi*. Bombay: Gandhi Book Centre, 1960.

Shridharani, Krishnalal. *The Mahatma and the World*. New York: Duell, Sloan and Pearce, 1946.

———. *War without Violence: A Study of Gandhi's Method and its Accomplishments*. New York: Brace Harcour,1939.

Singh, K.J. 'Gandhi and Mao as Mass Communicators.' *Journal of Communication* 24 (1979): 94–101.

Singh, M.P. 'Gandhi as Rebel.' *Gandhi Marg*, January–March (1996): 474–78.

Singh, Radhey Shyam. *The Constructive Programmes of Mahatma Gandhi (1920–1939)*. New Delhi: Commonwealth Publishers, 1991.

Sinha, Mrinalini. *Colonial Masculinity: The 'Manly Englishman' and the 'Effeminate Bengali' in the Late 19th Century*. New York: Manchester University Press, 1995.

Sofri, Gianni. *Gandhi and India*. Gloucestershire: The Windrush Press, 1999.

Suchak, Kavita. *Rural Industrialisation with Special Reference to 'Khadi'*. Mumbai: Yogesh Suchak, 1999.

Tarlo, Emma. *Clothing Matters, Dress and Identity in India*. Chicago: University of Chicago Press, 1996.

Tendulkar, D.G. *Mahatma*, Vols 1–8. Delhi: Publications Division, (1951–54), 1960.

Thakore, Dilip J. *Gandhian Era in Gujarati Literature*. Rajkot, Jyoti Prakashan, Mandir, 1955.

Tharoor, Shashi. *India, From Midnight to the Millennium.* New Delhi: Penguin Books, 2000.

Thomas, P.J. *Mercantilism and the East India Trade.* London: P.S. King & Son, (1926) 1963.

Thorat, Sukhadeo and Umakant, eds. *Caste, Race and Discrimination.* Jaipur: Rawat Publications, 2004.

Tikekar, S.R. *Epigrams from Gandhiji.* Ahmedabad: Navajivan, (1974) 1994.

Virmani, Arundhati. 'National Symbols under Colonial Domination: The Nationalization of the Indian Flag, March–August 1923.' *Past & Present* 164 (1999): 169–97.

Watson, John Forbes. *The Textile Manufactures and Costumes of the People of India.* London: G.E. Eyre & W. Spottiswoode, 1866.

Weber, Thomas. 'Gandhi's Salt March as Living Sermon.' *Gandhi Marg* 22 (4): 424–25, 2001.

———. *Gandhi, Gandhism and the Gandhians.* New Delhi: Roli Books, 2006.

———. *On the Salt March: The Historiography of Gandhi's March to Dandi.* New Delhi: HarperCollins, 1998.

Weiner, A. and J. Schneider, eds. *Cloth and Human Experience.* Washington: Smithsonian Institution Press, 1989.

Xavier, N.S. 'Gandhi and the Issue of Identity.' *Gandhi Marg*, December (1986): 520–39.

B. Communication Theories

Appadurai, Arjun, ed. *The Social Life of Things: Commodities in Cultural Perspective.* Cambridge: Cambridge University Press, 1986.

Argyle, Michael. *Bodily Communication.* London: Methuen, 1975.

———. *The Psychology of Interpersonal Behaviour.* London: Penguin, 1972.

Barringer, Tim and Tom Flynn, eds. *Colonialism and the Object, Empire, Material Culture and the Museum.* London: Routledge, 1998.

Barry, Ann Marie Steward. *Visual Intelligence: Perception, Image and Manipulation in Visual Communication.* New York: State University of New York Press, 1997.

Barthes, Roland. *Camera Lucida.* Translated by Richard Howard. London: Vintage, 2000.

———. *Elements of Semiology.* Translated by Annette Lavers and Colin Smith. New York: Hill and Wang, 1968.

———. *Image Music Text.* Translated by Stephen Heath. London: Fontana Press, 1977.

———. *Mythologies.* London: Paladin, 1973.

———. *S/Z.* Translated by Richard Miller. New York: Noonday, 1974.

———. *The Grain of the Voice: Interviews 1962–80.* Translated by Linda Coverdale. New York: Hill and Wang, 1985.

———. *The Fashion System.* Translated by Richard Howard and Matthew Ward. Berkeley: University of California Press, 1990.

Blumer, Herbert. *Symbolic Interactionism: Perspective and Method.* New Jersey: Prentice-Hall, 1969.

Blumer, Herbert. 'Fashion: From Class Differentiation to Collective Selection.' *The Sociological Quarterly* 10 (1969): 275–91.

Calefato, Patrizia. *The Clothed Body*, translated by Lisa Adams. Oxford, Washington: Berg, 2004.

Carlson, Marvin. *Performance: A Critical Introduction*. London: Routledge, 1996.

Carter, Michael. *Fashion Classics from Carlyle to Barthes*. Oxford: Berg, 2003.

Chandler, David. *Semiotics: The Basics*. New York: Routledge, 2002.

Cohn, Bernard S. *Colonialism and its Forms of Knowledge: The British in India*. New Jersey: Princeton University Press, 1996.

Counsell, Colin and Laurie Wolf. *Performance Analysis*. London: Routledge, 2001.

Eco, Umberto. *Trattato di Semiotica Generale*. Milano: Bompiani, 1994.

Ekman, P. and W. Friesen. 'The Repertoire of Nonverbal Behavior. Categories, Origins, Usage, and Coding.' *Semiotica* 1(1969): 49–98.

Evans, Jessica and Stuart Hall, eds. *Visual Culture: The Reader*. London: Sage Publications, 1999.

Flugel, J.C. *The Psychology of Clothes*. London: Hogart Press, 1930.

Forsythe, S. 'Effect of Applicant's Clothing on Interviewer's Decision to Hire.' *Journal of Applied Psychology*, 20 (1990): 1579–95.

Gandhi, Leela. *Postcolonial Theory: A Critical Introduction*. Columbia: University Press, 1998.

Gibbins, K. 'Communication Aspects of Women's Clothes and their Relation to Fashionability.' *British Journal of Social and Clinical Psychology* 8 (1969): 301–12.

Gibbins, K. and A. Schneider. 'Meaning of Garments: Relation between Impression of an Outfit and the Message Carried by its Components Garments' *Perceptual and Motor Skills* 51 (1980): 287–91.

Goffman, Erving. *Behavior in Public Places: Notes on the Social Organization of Gatherings*. New York: Free Press of Glencoe, 1963.

———. *Interaction Ritual: Essays on Face-to-Face Behavior*. New York: Doubleday, 1967.

———. *Strategic Interaction*. Pennsylvania: University of Pennsylvania Press, 1969.

———. *The Presentation of Self in Everyday Life*. New York: Anchor Books, 1959.

Hall, Edward T. *The Hidden Dimension: Man's Use of Space in Public and Private*. London: Bodley Head, 1966.

———. *The Silent Language*. New York: Anchor Books, 1973.

Hamid, P.N. 'Style of Dress as a Perceptual Cue in Impression Formation.' *Perceptual and Motor Skills* 26 (1968): 904–06.

Henley, Nancy M. *Body Politics*. New Jersey: Prentice-Hall, 1977.

Hetherington, Kevin. *Expressions of Identity: Space, Performance and Politics*. London: Sage Publications, 1998.

Hilton, Julian. *Performance*. London: MacMillan, 1987.

Hoult, R. 'Experimental Measurement of Clothing as a Factor in Some Social Ratings of Selected American Men' *American Sociological Reveiw* 19 (1954): 324–28.

Huxley, Michael and Noel Witts, eds. *The Twentieth Century Performance Reader*. London: Routledge, 1996.

Jasper, C.R. and M.E. Roach-Higgins, 'Role Conflict and Conformity in Dress.' *Social Behavior and Personality*, 16 (1988): 227–40.

Johnson, Kim K.P., Susan J. Torntore, and Joanne B. Eicher, eds. *Fashion Foundations: Early Writings on Fashion and Dress.* New York: Berg Publishers, 2003.

Kerr, B.A. and D.M. Dell 'Perceived Interviewer Expertness and Attractiveness: Effect of Interviewer Behaviour and Attire and Interview Setting.' *Journal of Counseling Psychology* 23(1976): 553–56.

Knox L.A. and J.C. Mancuso 'Incongruities in self-presentations and Judgments about People' *Perceptual and Motor Skills* 52 (1981): 843–52.

Kress, G. *Communication and Culture: An introduction.* Kensington: New South Wales University Press, 1988.

Lapitsky, Mary. 'Impact of Clothing on Impressions of Personal Characteristics and Writing Ability.' *Family and Consumer Sciences Research Journal* 9 (1981): 327–35.

Leeds-Hurwitz, Wendy. *Semiotics and Communication: Signs, Codes, Cultures.* New Jersey: Lawrence Erlbaum Associates, 1993.

Lemert, Charles and Ann Branaman, eds. *The Goffman Reader,* Massachusetts: Blackwell, 1997.

Lurie, Alison. *The Language of Clothes.* New York: Owl Books, 2000.

Munns, Jessica and Penny Richards, eds. *The Clothes that Wear Us: Essays on Dressing and Transgressing in Eighteenth-century Culture.* Newark: University of Delaware Press, 1999.

Oommen, T.K. 'Erving Goffman and Study of Everyday Protest.' In *Alien Concepts and South Asian Reality: Responses and Reformulations,* edited by T.K. Oommen, 170–88. New Delhi: Sage Publications, 1995.

Pratt, M.L. *Imperial Eyes: Travel Writing and Transculturation.* New York: Routledge, 1992.

Riggins, Stephen Harold. *Beyond Goffman: Studies on Communication, Institution, and Social Interaction.* New York: Mouton de Gruyter, 1990.

Sage, Stephanine John. 'Eliminating the distance: From Barthes' Écriture-Lecture to Écriture-vue.' In *Cultural Semiosis: Tracing the Signifier,* edited by Hugh J. Silverman, 105–28. London: Routledge, 1998.

Said, Edward. *Culture and Imperialism.* London: Chatto & Windus, 1993.

———. *Orientalism.* Harmondsworth: Penguin, 2003.

Scalmer, Sean. 'Turner Meets Gandhi: Pilgrimage, Ritual, and the Diffusion of Nonviolent Direct Action.' In *Victor Turner and Contemporary Cultural Performance*, edited by Graham St. John, New York: Berghahn Books, 2005.

Schechner, Richard. *Performance Studies: An Introduction.* New York: Routledge, 2002.

———. *Performance Theory.* New York: Routledge, 2003.

Smith, G., ed. *Goffman and Social Organization: Studies in a Sociological Legacy.* London: Routhledge, 1999.

Steele, Valerie. *Encyclopaedia of Clothing and Fashion.* Detroit: Charles Scribner's Sons, 2004.

Stone, G.P. 'Appearance and the Self.' In *Human Behavior and Social Processes,* edited by A.M. Rose, 86–118, London: Routledge & Keagan, 1962.

Turner, Victor. *Dramas, Fields and Metaphors: Symbolic Action in Human Society.* Ithaca: Cornell University Press, 1974.

———. *From Ritual to Theatre.* New York: Performing Arts Journal Publications, 1982.

Turner, Victor. *Image and Pilgrimage in Christian Culture: Anthropological Perspectives.* New York: Columbia University Press, 1978.

———. *The Anthropology of Performance.* New York: PAJ Publications, 1988.

———. *The Forest of Symbols.* Ithaca: Cornell University Press, 1986.

———. *The Ritual Process: Structure and Anti-structure.* Chicago: Aldine Publishing Co., 1969.

Turner-Bowker, Diane M. 'How Can You Pull Yourself Up by Your Bootstraps, if You Don't Have Boots? Work-Appropriate Clothing for Poor Women.' *Journal of Social Issues* 57 (2001): 311–22.

Wiemann John and Randall Harrison. *Nonverbal Interaction.* New Delhi: Sage Publications, 1983.

Index

About the Author

Peter Gonsalves, PhD, currently teaches the Sciences of Social Communication at Salesian Pontifical University, Rome.

He began his career in media as a community worker for rural development at the Bosco Gramin Vikas Kendra, Ahmednagar. He founded Tej-prasarini, Mumbai, a multimedia production centre to raise awareness of the urgency of life-based education in South Asia. He promoted a series of teacher-training manuals called 'Quality Life Education', the first of which was his own work: *Exercises in Media Education* (1994). Using this, he conducted no less than 40 all-India courses on media education for schoolteachers, social workers and youth facilitators form diverse ethnic, cultural and religious backgrounds.

Dr Gonsalves is a member of the Salesians of Don Bosco, an international society dedicated to the holistic development of young people. He coordinated its first five-language web portal at its headquarters in Rome. He was also president of INTERSIG, the international wing of SIGNIS, a world association of communicators for a culture of peace.